Literary Federalism in the
Age of Jefferson

Literary Federalism in the Age of Jefferson

Joseph Dennie and
The Port Folio, 1801–1812

William C. Dowling

University of South Carolina Press

Published in Columbia, South Carolina, by the
University of South Carolina Press

Manufactured in the United States of America

03 02 01 00 99   5 4 3 2 1

Library of Congress Cataloging-in-Publication Data

Dowling, William C.
    Literary federalism in the age of Jefferson : Joseph Dennie and
The port folio, 1801–1812 / William C. Dowling.
      p. cm.
    Includes bibliographical references and index.
    ISBN 1-57003-243-2
    1. Dennie, Joseph, 1768–1812—Political and social views.
2. Politics and literature—United States—History—19th century.
3. Authors, American—19th century—Political and social views.
4. Federal government—United States—History—19th century.
5. American literature—1783–1850—History and criticism.   6. United
States—Politics and government—1801–1809.   7. United States—
Politics and government—1809–1817.   8. Jefferson, Thomas,
1743–1826—In literature.   9. American periodicals—History—19th
century.   10. Port folio.   I. Title.
PS1534.D6D69   1999
814'.2—dc21   97-45469

For Quentin Anderson

Contents

Preface

THIS book is about the literary opposition to Thomas Jefferson in the early years of the American republic, in particular in *The Port Folio* magazine edited by Joseph Dennie out of Philadelphia between 1801 and 1811. It concentrates on an unremarked episode, the gradual withdrawal of the Federalist writers from overt political opposition to Jefferson into a specific realm of literary or aesthetic values, as though the Federalism of such men as Alexander Hamilton and John Adams, having been banished from the realm of politics, had then found sanctuary in a separate sphere of writing where it survived as a mode of literary expression. *Literary Federalism in the Age of Jefferson* thus attempts both to analyze what Louis Simpson has called "the paradoxical, complex estrangement of American men of letters from the Revolution and the new nation" ("Symbolism" 82) and to account for the genesis of a distinct and important strain in American thought and writing.

To read through *The Port Folio* during the years of Dennie's editorship is to find oneself in the very midst of what I shall be calling the Federalist retreat from history, a long and complex withdrawal in which Federalism, banished from the civic sphere by a triumphant Jeffersonian ideology, seeks an alternative home in what we now call the public sphere but what the *Port Folio* writers called, in the usual eighteenth-century phrase, the republic of letters. By the end of the process, as we shall see, literary Federalism will have emerged as such through its powerful imaginative identification with the late-Augustan milieu of Johnson and Goldsmith and Burke in England, a literary world itself sustained amid a clamorous modernity by its memory of traditional or organic society. This is the period during which Oliver Goldsmith became the tutelary spirit of literary Federalism, presiding over a mode in American writing originating in *The Port Folio* and bequeathed by Dennie in his last years to his young protégé Washington Irving in New York.

The protagonist of the story of literary Federalism is *The Port Folio* itself, entering as the collective consciousness or voice of Federalism into unremitting ideological warfare against Jeffersonian democracy. The normal eighteenth-century convention of an editorial persona— "Oliver Oldschool," discussed in chapter 2 as the imaginary or collective voice of Federalist values—has accordingly seemed to me to demand a mode of phenomenological reading, taking *The Port Folio* as a self-contained universe of discourse that asks the reader to look outward from its own literary horizon upon the crowded scene of the early American republic. This demands a certain adjustment of historical perspective. Thus it is, for instance, that from inside the world of *The Port Folio* another important Federalist publication like the *New England Palladium* will be heard only as a distant sympathetic voice and someone like Fisher Ames, monumentally significant in his own right as the last great systematic Federalist thinker, only as a remote figure on the stage of national politics.

To read *The Port Folio* on what I am calling phenomenological terms is to listen to a complex medley of Federalist voices rising and falling in tones varying from genial urbanity to passionate political urgency, while in the background a great sweep of events carries Europe through the Napoleonic wars and the young American republic through an unexampled geographical expansion to an uneasy consolidation of constitutional rule. "The triumphing of Jefferson's party will be but short," Oliver Oldschool confidently predicts as *The Port Folio* begins its campaign of resistance in 1801. "Men will wake from the dreams of apathy, and the darkness of delusion" (1:262). Yet even in these early days one may in the pages of *The Port Folio* already sense the tremors given off by the tectonic shift in the foundations of history that will, by the time of Dennie's early death in 1812, have permanently extinguished Federalism as a living force in American politics.

For students of American history, the losing battle fought by political Federalism against Jeffersonian ideology is merely an episode in a larger national story that ends thirty years later in the full-blown triumph of Jacksonian backwoods democracy and the common man. For students of American literature, however, the Federalist retreat from history has somewhat different implications. For the triumph of

Jeffersonian ideology in politics, leading to a corresponding interpretation of American literature as finally and triumphally "democratic"—of Emerson, for instance, as the prophetic voice of a limitless American potentiality, or Melville as novelist of the people and the world of ordinary work, or Whitman as the inspired singer of visionary democracy and the sovereign nation—has left us with no real way to account for a major feature of American writing, that pronounced estrangement or alienation Richard Poirier had in mind in speaking of American literature as a "world elsewhere," a deliberate attempt to create in language an alternative to the conditions of American social existence.

Nearly seventy years ago, Matthew Josephson argued in *A Portrait of the Artist as American* that the most truly American writer is the one who has felt most acutely the sense of belonging "to another age or climate," and that this feeling was rooted in a deep unspoken suspicion that the real story of American society has been one of "unstable democracy, of herd-life, of the unbridled passion for gain, of decline in the human and political arts" (xvi). To see such an argument as even possibly true is at least to imagine the possibility of an alternative story about American literature in which such writers as Emerson and Whitman would appear less as heroic voices of a visionary democracy than as figments of a peculiarly American ideology, and Melville not as democratic novelist but the writer whom Josephson describes as living out an obscure tragedy in a country that did not want his genius: "doomed, uncomprehending, hating the age, he wandered in the anonymous crowd, resigned to his disappearance from the world; he is a sphinx-like figure, living for thirty years in a tomb" (xxi).

The epigraph Josephson chose for *A Portrait of the Artist as American* is a sentence taken from Melville in the long period of his last loneliness: "I feel I am an exile here." The same sentence might be taken as the watchword of an important strain in American writing that extends from the age of Washington Irving to the time of Henry Adams and Santayana, a tradition that very often does include the actual emigration or exile of American writers but which begins in a deeper sense of literature itself as a spiritual exile from the conditions of American democracy. It is the presence of this hidden or repressed tradition in American writing, it seems to me, that lends a special significance to that moment in the early American republic when Joseph Dennie and *The Port Folio*, realizing that the battle they have been losing is not against Thomas Jefferson but America itself, turn away from politics and civic controversy to literature as a world elsewhere.

My larger argument in the following pages will be that the origins of this estrangement of certain important American writers from

America are to be discovered in the moment that Federalism vanished from the political sphere to be reborn as a mode of literary expression. But there is an embarrassment here, for this is also necessarily to acknowledge that the triumph of Jeffersonian democracy brought with it a certain blockage or repression in the way we have conceived of our national literary past, something resembling a taboo in its power to impose silences and regulate perceptions. Taking the Federalist retreat from history seriously means, in short, trying to understand why so much subsequent American writing has felt compelled to create a world in language that might serve as a conscious alternative to what a character in Henry James calls the crude and garish climate of American civilization. The ruling taboo here is, one comes to see, against any account of American cultural emptiness—ugliness, mindlessness, garishness—that might portray this emptiness as an inevitable consequence of democracy in the civic sphere. One may hint at this failure obliquely, observing with James that "the soil of American perception is a poor little barren artificial deposit," or with Santayana that in America "the moral soil is too thin and shifting" to nourish genuine art, but, having done so, one's wisest course is perhaps, as the cases of both James and Santayana suggest, to emigrate.

To understand why this strain of literary skepticism about democracy has been repressed in our own century in favor of a more suitably "democratic" tradition of writing, it is perhaps only necessary to recall that modern American literary studies came to birth in an intellectual climate dominated by the Progressive historians, most notably Charles Beard and Harry Elmer Barnes, Progressive history being, to an extent we have only now begun to appreciate, the belated triumph of Jeffersonian or Jacksonian ideology in American historiography. This is an ideology already at work when, in the following chapters, we will hear the Jeffersonian adversaries of *The Port Folio* muttering balefully that Federalism, with its talk about civic virtue and devotion to classical values, is nothing more than an "aristocratical" conspiracy of the wealthy and educated against the impoverished and ignorant. In the same way, one may hear Andrew Jackson a quarter century later, at the time of the Bank War, warning ominously that by "a silent and secret operation" control is being "exercised by the few over the political conduct of the many" (qtd. in Meyers 14). This strain then culminates in our own century when a work like Beard's *Economic Interpretation of the Constitution* (1913) is able to offer a similar story about a privileged elite or monied aristocracy as a serious explanation of early republican history.

The aims of Beard and his school have been greatly illuminated recently by Ernst Breisach's *American Progressive History*, one virtue of which, for students of American literature, is the strong light it sheds on Vernon Parrington. For in *Main Currents of American Thought*, as Breisach makes clear, Parrington thought of himself as undertaking in literary history a task identical to that being carried out by Beard and Barnes and James Harvey Robinson in social and economic history. This may be taken to explain, one suspects, what a reader of *Main Currents* even today experiences as a certain ferocious integrity on Parrington's part. It is fashionable nowadays to dismiss Parrington out of hand for the crudity or tendentiousness of his opinions, but his work nonetheless has great value for understanding certain tendencies still visible in the study of American literature. Nowhere do we see as clearly what American literature looks like when viewed from an unapologetically Jeffersonian or Jacksonian perspective.

One is thus able in *Main Currents* to watch what I have been calling the repression of literary Federalism being carried out as part of Parrington's wholly conscious campaign against all vestiges of "aristocratical" thought in American culture, every trace of the older attitude that had favored property and education and classical values over mere numerical democracy as a basis of civic governance. One need only read Parrington's discussion of Timothy Dwight or Joseph Dennie today, for instance, to understand why in the aftermath of *Main Currents* the Federalist writers would simply vanish from anthologies of American literature. In the same way, it is possible to extrapolate from Parrington's discussion of John Adams an entire way of looking at American literature. Here is Parrington describing what he honestly believes to be Adams's beliefs about society and human nature:

> The universal social state is one of ruthless class struggle, wherein the strong conquer the weak. . . . It cannot be otherwise, he argued, from the natural inequality of men. The rude mass being shiftless, ignorant, spendthrift, they are at the mercy of the strong, ambitious, and capable, who exploit them freely. Hence in every society emerges the division between patricians and plebeians, developing into caste as the social order grows complex. The self-interest of the patricians teaches them the need of class solidarity, and with intelligent solidarity the few easily seize control of the state and use it to their ends. Hence arises an aristocracy or oligarchy, which maintains its power through control of the economic resources of society. Control of property means control of men; for sovereignty inheres in economics. (313)

To read Parrington's account of Thomas Jefferson, by the same token, is to be given in a few sentences the key to his exaltation of that entire tradition to which Larzar Ziff has given the name literary democracy. For Jefferson in Parrington's eyes is a figure less out of history than allegory, a shining spirit backed by "the philosophy of a new age and a new people. . . . More completely than any other American of his generation, he embodied the idealisms of the great revolution—its faith in human nature, its economic individualism, its conviction that here in America, through the instrumentality of political democracy, the lot of the common man should somehow be made better" (343). It is not Parrington's voice alone that one hears at such moments, but, in literary history, the voice of Van Wyck Brooks and F. O. Matthiessen and a thousand lesser-known students of American literature, including the authors of books being published today. It is, at the national or collective level, the voice of Jeffersonian democracy as the American ideology.

The wellspring of Federalist resistance to Jeffersonian democracy, as we shall see, is the classical republican notion of civic virtue as a mode of disinterestedness, a willingness to live in and for one's community rather than oneself. One way of marking the vast historical divide that separates us from the Federalists is to say that the term literary Federalism as it occurs in my title would have made no sense to those who thought of themselves as Federalists at the moment of the Jeffersonian ascendancy. For the essence of Federalism as a civic vision—what gives it today the status nearly of a lost or forgotten body of thought—is that it belonged to a time before there was any presumed divorce or separation between literary and civic values. A still more decisive breach dividing us from the Federalist generation is the shift in the meaning of the very word "democracy." For such men as Hamilton and Ames and Dennie were at one in understanding "democracy" in its classical or Aristotelian sense—as a degeneration of governance into rule by the *demos*, the unstable multitude or mob—and were thus united in a passionate conviction that Jeffersonian democracy was nothing other than American "jacobinism," a word indissolubly associated in their minds with Robespierre and the recent reign of blood and terror in revolutionary France.

Only now, perhaps, two hundred years further on, when the revolutionary inheritance of blood and terror has darkened the lives of innumerable millions around the world, does the Federalist detestation of jacobinism seem reasonable rather than (as could be said before Stalin and Mao and Pol Pot) reactionary. Only now, when thinkers like Michael Sandel, Robert Bellah, and Charles Taylor have found it once

xiv

again possible to argue that (in Taylor's words) "the republican thesis is as relevant and true today as it was in ancient or early modern times, when the paradigms of civic humanism were articulated" (197), are we in a position to understand the urgency with which Joseph Dennie and the *Port Folio* writers warned that the whole Jeffersonian idealization of the common man—"the philosophy of a new age and a new people"— was mystification merely, an attempt to mask an order driven by unbridled self-interest and crude economic individualism in a noble rhetoric of universal human dignity. In the urgency of that warning begins the story that will end, as we shall see, in the Federalist retreat from history into the sanctuary of literary or aesthetic consciousness.

The earliest draft of this book was written when I was a visiting Fulbright lecturer on American literature at the Universidad Autónoma de Madrid in 1992–1993. Patricia Zahniser of the Comisión de Intercambio Cultural and Lorenzo Rodríguez Durántez of the Asociación J. William Fulbright went to special lengths to make that year in Spain a delight, and I thank them. For the friendship and support of Gema Chocano Díaz and Victor Santiago Menéndez Martinez my debt goes beyond gratitude; *no tengo palabras adecuadas para expresárlo*, and I shall not try.

At Rutgers, three valued colleagues in American literature— Richard Poirier, Myra Jehlen, and Michael Warner—have been a continuous source of energy and inspiration. My debt to Joyce Appleby is equally great. Every reader of the following pages will see how central her work has been to my own thinking about the early American republic. What the reader cannot see is how enormously helpful her generous and perceptive comments were at a crucial stage of the writing. I am also grateful to Christopher Looby for helpful comments on several important points of presentation. Conversations with a number of friends and colleagues—Lance Banning, Peter Berkowitz, Leo Damrosch, Linda Dowling, Thomas Edwards, Russell Goodman, Richard Howard, Thomas Pavel, John Pocock, Jackson Lears, Colin Wells—influenced the argument at various points, and I thank them. Finally, my thinking about the literary opposition to Jeffersonian democracy began in, and over the years has been guided by, conversations with Quentin Anderson; a sense of my gratitude is imperfectly registered in the dedication to this volume.

Chapter One

The Demon Democracy

IN April 1803, there appeared in *The Port Folio*, the nation's earliest important journal of political and literary opinion, an angry denunciation of democracy in Jeffersonian America. Its author was Joseph Dennie, a Harvard-educated lawyer who had abandoned his legal prospects in Walpole, New Hampshire—exchanging "lone quiet, and deep forests," as he put it, "for the ever varying scenes of active life; fumum, opes, strepitumque Romae"[1]—to come to Philadelphia, where he would gain an almost immediate national visibility as the presiding spirit of *The Port Folio*. "The Editor," Dennie wrote some years later, "came here as a stranger and pilgrim"; "Philadelphia has adopted him as her own" (7:1:278). During those years, Dennie would voice innumerable strong opinions about Jeffersonian democracy, but this one fugitive paragraph has a special status. It provided the grounds on which he would be arraigned for seditious libel, an attempt actually to bring down the government of Thomas Jefferson and those already calling themselves "democratic republicans."

To modern ears, for which the word democracy carries wholly positive connotations, Dennie's denunciations of Jeffersonian democracy have seemed driven by some mysterious private animus. Several of Dennie's pronouncements, a modern commentator on *The Port Folio* goes so far as to say, thinking of the paragraph for which Dennie would be summoned into court as a factious and seditious person, actually have about them "the ring of insanity" (Queenan 120). The offending paragraph runs, in part, as follows: "A democracy is scarcely tolerable at any period of national history. Its omens are always sinister. . . . It was weak and wicked in Athens. It was bad in Sparta, and worse in Rome. It has been tried in France, and has terminated in despotism. It was tried in England, and rejected with the utmost loathing and abhorrence. It is on its trial here, and the issue will be civil war, desolation, and anarchy" (3:135).

This is not, as anyone familiar with the work of Pocock and others will immediately recognize, insanity. It is an ancient language of the polity whose most basic assumptions go back to Aristotle's *Politics*. Yet the fact that a modern reader of *The Port Folio* was able only a few short years ago to imagine Dennie as being somehow in the grip of psychosis may serve to demonstrate how utterly the universe of political thought to which Dennie's vocabulary belongs was obliterated by the ideological triumph of French revolutionary ideas in Europe and Jeffersonian democracy in America. Nonetheless, on both sides of the Atlantic, under the tremendous pressure of events in revolutionary France, that system of assumptions would be brought to a last eloquent expression by those who saw themselves as standing up against a debased modernity. Thus, when Dennie speaks of "a democracy," he will be speaking just the same language as Edmund Burke in England at about the same time, reminding his listeners of Aristotle's dictum that "an absolute democracy is not to be reckoned among the legitimate forms of government. It is the corruption and degeneracy, and not the sound constitution of a republic" (5:263).

In the earlier eighteenth century, the vocabulary used by Dennie and Burke would have been immediately recognized as belonging not simply to Aristotelian political theory but to such later transmutations of it as Polybius's theory of the mixed or balanced state, which for eighteenth-century Americans had survived most compellingly in Montesquieu's admiration for the mixed orders of the English constitution, and of the cyclical theory of history, according to which, once a sound republic has decomposed into the irrational turbulence of mob rule, democracy inevitably produces tyranny in the person of a single strong ruler (a Caesar, a Cromwell, a Napoleon) who reimposes order on the anarchy of the state. This language was already passing away when Joseph Dennie sat down to write his bleak assessment of American democracy in *The Port Folio*, but it was, fortunately for him, not yet forgotten by the judge presiding at his trial. The jury must acquit the defendant, declared Judge Yeates in his charge, so long as Dennie's "supposed censures on democracy" might be taken to refer to "pure unmixed democracy, where the people en masse execute the sovereign power without the medium of their representatives" (Queenan 124).

The special poignancy of the Aristotelian or Polybian vocabulary used by Dennie is that it was for him, as for his fellow Federalists during these perplexed years, simply a neutral and uncontroversial way of describing the American republic as it really and recently seemed to them to have existed in the golden era of Washington's governance, an America enshrined in the checks and balances, so obviously inspired by the wisdom of Aristotle and Polybius and Montesquieu, of the written Constitution. This is why Dennie is able so spontaneously to use the Polybian language of cyclical forms—the wheel of history moving inexorably through democratic anarchy to the tyrant's rule—in pointing again and again to France under Napoleon as a monitory parable for Jeffersonian America: "France has reached her last stage of revolutionary insanity. The people are in a state of vassalage. Government is vested, by violence, in a revolutionary despot. . . . The revolutionary wheel went round . . . revolving to the tremendous despotism of a military upstart" (5:231).

To recall that revolution even in the early nineteenth century retained strong associations with cyclical theory—the cycle of forms within particular states, the great cycle of historical process, what the English poet Dyer called "the revolving course of mighty time," as it explained the rise and fall of civilizations like Greece and Rome—is to recall that for most Americans of Dennie's generation their own revolution was an event demanding to be understood in cyclical terms, the *ricorso* of classical republican political theory as it brought into being an American republic that was, in effect, a younger, more virtuous England freed from the corruption of Hanoverian Britain.[2] As historians like Joyce Appleby and James Rogers Sharp have demonstrated,[3] it was their sense of themselves as custodians of this vision that makes Federalists like Dennie and Fisher Ames the classical republicans of the early federal era, ceaselessly combating the attempt of Jefferson and his party to take over the idiom of classical republican thought for opposing purposes. The object of political wisdom, for Dennie and *The Port Folio* writers, was simply to preserve the America one had so miraculously been given. Here, in the pages of *The Port Folio*, is a Federalist judge addressing a grand jury in Pennsylvania on the eve of Jefferson's presidency:

> Favored . . . with a happy republican system, and administration of government, we participate in its powers, and are protected in our persons, property, character, and conscience. And favored with a fertile soil, and not inclement climate, we have the means of health and prosperity, and the hopes of rearing our children to a greater enjoyment of all those blessings, and transmitting them, with increased advantage, to our posterity. We may be happy if we will be so. . . . But alas, what is man! and how is it that the human heart is always corrupted by prosperity! When God has furnished us with all provision for contentment, we disquiet ourselves with vain cares, and false suspicions, and turn our best blessings into a curse and a calamity. (1:154)

The reason that the history of past civilizations remains so unerring a source of wisdom about the present—"It was bad in Sparta," we recall Dennie saying about democracy, "and worse in Rome"—is, for Federalists like Dennie and Ames, that there remains constant in every human society that principle of irrationality, of pure egoistic self-gratification, that in ancient political theory was always embodied in the uncontrolled *demos* or *vulgus*, the people viewed under the aspect of mob or crowd response. "Non est consilium in vulgo, non ratio," Cicero had said, and the identical thought is in the mind of the writer in *The New England Palladium* who, in a piece reprinted in *The Port Folio*, says that, while he is the last person in the world "to desire to strip the people of all power, for then slavery would ensue," that nonetheless "their uncontrolled power is despotism, in its least hopeful form" (3:137). The complicating factor is that the demos from Aristotle onwards is normally portrayed in terms of higher and lower social status, so that to modern ears what seems to be at issue is some unfathomable ground of class antagonism. Thus, for instance, the strangeness for the modern reader of *The Port Folio*'s frequent fulminations against "turbulent demagogues, and beer house politicians" (1:38), or of *The Deserted Dram Shop*, a satiric version of Goldsmith's *The Deserted Village* adjusted to the squalid new reality of Jefferson's America:

> A time there was, ere demos rul'd the state,
> When there they met to tipple and debate;
> For them the candidate his rum would pour,
> Give just enough to lay them on the floor; . . .
> But times are chang'd, new rulers are elected,
> And drunkards now for honors are selected. . . .
> These all to Monticello now have flown,
> And left the landlord to get drunk alone. (5:8)

There is a further complication. In Federalist writing, the Aristotelian vocabulary of higher and lower social status sometimes takes on a kind of sociological literalness, which is what then allows their Jeffersonian adversaries to denounce "aristocratical" tendencies within Federalism. Yet the great paradox is that *The Port Folio* feels free to use a language of higher and lower rank only because Federalism had so completely accepted what Gordon Wood has called the radicalism of the American Revolution. To the Federalist writers, the revolutionary move of abolishing aristocracy and inherited privilege in America seemed self-evidently to have opened up a kind of mobility unknown in the older states of Europe, the very point of which was to allow such qualities as intelligence and personal energy to lead to increased prosperity and social status. In the pages of *The Port Folio*, the new American republic exists as the unexampled instance of a social domain in which moral attitudes—industry and foresight, for instance, as opposed to indolence and present gratification—really do manifest themselves over time as a difference in social status.

For all that, *The Port Folio*'s impatience with beer-house politicians has essentially to do not with social status as such but, as with similar dismissals of the lower orders in Aristotle and Plato, with moral psychology, the idea of a "higher" and "lower" self in perpetual conflict, internal to the human condition in every age and culture. To see the demos as the lowest order in the state is simply to see that it corresponds at the level of collective thought and action to the lower self of Greek ethical thought and Judeo-Christian theology—the Augustinian or fallen self that has the alcoholic reaching for the drink he knows will destroy him even though he is rationally convinced that he is ruining his life. Behind the portrayal of the demos in Aristotle or Polybius or the speeches of Fisher Ames lies Socrates' equation of the individual moral constitution and the constitution of the state, behind which in turn lies Plato's great metaphor of the human soul as a charioteer struggling upwards toward the sun while dragged constantly back to earth by its lower desires. The beer-house politicians of *The Deserted Dram Shop* are there not because the Federalists imagine that the lower orders drink themselves into insensibility while the upper orders remain primly sober, but because the dram shop is where any of us, given a certain inescapable human weakness, might expect to encounter our own worst selves.

Nonetheless, the moral urgency of *The Port Folio*'s warfare against Thomas Jefferson arises from its bleak sense that in America in 1801 there are at work forces never dreamt of in the Athens of Pericles or the Rome of Caesar and Cicero, mysterious energies of social transformation that are in some uncanny sense impersonal, molding men and women and institutions in ways that do not answer to explanation in terms of individual intent or design. Today, when we are ourselves inclined to view these energies as belonging to a new money or market society just then beginning to emerge as a force of global transformation, Federalist writing seems curiously clairvoyant, always at least attempting to understand the French Revolution and Jeffersonian democracy as expressions of some as-yet-ungraspable system of economic relations that compel one to view events at home and in distant London or Paris as exerting simultaneous influence on one another. Yet the system, for all the visibility of such effects as the storming of the

Bastille or the election of Thomas Jefferson to the American presidency, remained uncanny, and for that reason deeply threatening.

The *Port Folio* writers understood as well that this system of social and economic relations, whatever else it might turn out to be, was a new and powerful ideological system, ominously threatening to annihilate Federalism and the surviving tradition of classical republican thought through the specific means of reconsecrating the demos of Aristotelian theory as "the people," the spurious source of a supposedly inexhaustible civic virtue. This is what Alexander Hamilton means when, in an address prominently featured in *The Port Folio*, he warns his listeners that the contest between Federalism and Jeffersonian democracy "is, indeed, a war of principles": "It is a contest between the tyranny of jacobinism, which confounds and levels every thing, and the mild reign of rational liberty, which rests on the basis of a . . . well-balanced government, and through the medium of stable laws, shelters, and protects, the life, the reputation, the prosperity, the civic and religious rights, of every member of the community" (1:179).

Thomas Jefferson emerges for the *Port Folio* writers as a symbolic figure precisely because they are so convinced that dark or mysterious energies of social transformation are at work in the background of his political ascendancy. The very act of taking Jefferson as their symbol, thereby bestowing on modernity at least a visible presence and a recognizable voice, is for the Federalist writers a means of coming to terms with forces otherwise impersonal and unfathomable. The great modern prototype of this kind of writing, constantly present to the minds of Dennie and the *Port Folio* writers, had been the ideological warfare of the Augustan satirists against Sir Robert Walpole and his Robinocracy.[4] During the period of their active political opposition to Jefferson, the *Port Folio* writers normally viewed their own contributions as Augustan in this sense, literary language as a mode of symbolic action meant to alter the course of history, Jefferson as the visible embodiment of invisible forces of social disintegration or decline.[5]

Jefferson has always seemed the least likely of candidates for the role of grand symbolic antagonist, being as he was uncombative and detached, often apparently oblivious to the ideological furor raging around him. Yet this to the *Port Folio* writers was overwhelming evidence that they were right in their estimate of Jefferson as a metaphysician who had somehow wandered into the domain of practical politics, intensifying in his wide-eyed entrancement with visionary theories the consequences of forces elsewhere laying waste and desolation to vast tracts of the historical landscape. Jefferson was, in short, one of those philosophical doctors of the rights of man against whom

6

Burke had thundered so eloquently in *Reflections on the Revolution in France*, harmless enough in their closets but dangerous when allowed to put their theories to work in the world of actual human beings. Jefferson's rule, says Dennie in an early *Port Folio*, will be "the administration of a philosopher" (1:262), and the philosophy he has in mind is that of Reason and the Rights of Man.

At his least threatening, Jefferson appears in the pages of *The Port Folio* as a relatively harmless visionary, which is how Dennie is viewing him when he refers to Jefferson, as he recurrently does, as "the American Condorcet." For Condorcet is at such moments the boundlessly optimistic social philosopher of the *Tableau historique des progrès de l'esprit humain*, full of Rousseauian notions of natural innocence and Enlightenment theories of inevitable progress, giving voice to that entrancing fable of human perfectibility inside history that would be his great legacy to the progressive theorists of the nineteenth century, from Saint-Simon to Karl Marx to the Fabian Socialists. We glimpse the dark or demonic side of this same picture, what Dennie has in mind in speaking of *The Port Folio*'s war against Jeffersonianism as "a struggle with the baleful powers of hell and democracy" (1:262), only when we recall that Condorcet, having completed the *Tableau* and been denounced by the Jacobins, would die in prison at Bourg-la-Reine, one of the earliest of her children to be devoured by the Revolution.

The name given to Jeffersonian democracy by those who opposed Jefferson on these terms was "American jacobinism," made current by William Cobbett in his Peter Porcupine phase and then universally taken over in Federalist writing during Jefferson's presidency. On one level, this use of "jacobin" is to be explained by the unblushing sympathy of many Jeffersonians for French revolutionary ideas after the Revolution had taken its fatal turn to blood and Terror, and even after the subsequent rise of Napoleon to an autocratic power within the state unknown by the most absolute monarchs of the *ancien régime*. This is what gave such occurrences as the progress of Citizen Genet, for instance, toasted and wildly cheered by American democrats from Charleston to New York, an ominous symbolic significance in the eyes of later Federalist writers.[6] At a deeper level, however, the Federalist obsession with jacobinism has to do with their sense of the Revolution and the Terror as events generated by abstract ideas, false or visionary theories that had somehow been allowed to take on flesh-and-blood force in the domain of the real. This was modernity in its demonic aspect, something lying beyond the reach of analogies with ancient Greece or Rome.

The real enemy of the *Port Folio* writers is thus not Jefferson but ja-cobinism, the "foul fiend" the Federalist writers see as having flour-ished in Europe, especially in France and Germany, long before taking on visible shape in the French Revolution: "Its hideous features may be plainly discovered . . . in the multifarious works, profound and super-ficial, . . . in poetry and prose, of the numerous philosophists who del-uged both countries with their publications, during the latter half of the last century" (2:336). "The authors of the French Encyclopedia," says "An American, Resident Abroad" (John Quincy Adams) in 1801, "were the founders of a political and anti-religious sect, the object of which has been, to overthrow the Christian faith, and all the ancient estab-lishments of Europe. This undertaking . . . they accomplished in France, where they seated themselves, at least for a time, upon the ruins of the altar and throne they had destroyed" (1:179). The real war of *The Port Folio* is with the demonic visage of Enlightenment rational-ism itself, and with the philosophers or philosophes—"the Condorcets, the Wollstonecrafts, the Jeffersons, the Paines and the Godwins," as one *Port Folio* writer enumerates them (6:1:167)—only as they have vol-unteered as its agents or servants.

The Port Folio's grand strategy in the symbolic warfare against Jef-fersonian ideology thus becomes one of unmasking, dispelling the mists of visionary theory and "darkness of delusion" (1:262) in order to restore America to the sunlit world of peace and order and prosperity it had so recently known under Washington. The war now is between the ancient wisdom embodied in Aristotle and Cicero and Tacitus and jacobinism as the body of false doctrine that had produced the French Revolution, those arts, as one *Port Folio* writer puts it, through which "the infidel sophists of France" had created the conditions of possibil-ity for Robespierre and the Terror: "The minds of the people were poi-soned, they were taught to trample on the religion of their fathers, to believe, that death is an eternal sleep; before they were employed as the instruments of massacre, of universal plunder and devastation" (1:180). This is the context in which such Federalist periodicals as *The Port Folio* and *The New England Palladium* will issue forth as champions of truth and sanity in a war against error and mystification,[7] and in which Dennie in his role as editor of *The Port Folio* will describe "philo-sophical encounters" as contests which may be "as bloody as the bat-tles of Bonaparte" (6:2:82).

To hear *The Port Folio* speak, as it once does, of the "false politics, false logic, and false metaphysics" even of Jefferson's Declaration of Independence (1:20)—a document, one might otherwise assume, honorably enough associated with its own vision of America as a virtuous republic—is thus to understand its attempt to isolate Jefferson as the anomalous source of radical French ideas in an otherwise sane context of classical republican values, to expose as visionary one or another of those false doctrines that in France have already brought about desolation and ruin. The most fundamental of these doctrines, perhaps, is that notion of innate or natural virtue now commonly spoken of as the new Pelagianism of eighteenth-century thought (see Passmore). The remoter origins of this idea lie, as was normally recognized in the eighteenth century, in the work of the third earl of Shaftesbury and, through him, in Cambridge Platonism; as a doctrine of the European Enlightenment, it is indissolubly associated with the thought of Rousseau, particularly during the period of *Émile* and the *Contrat Social*.

To Americans of the revolutionary generation, the ethical thought of Shaftesbury was most compellingly available within the tradition of Scots moral sense theory, the line that runs from Shaftesbury's *Characteristics* through Hutcheson to Adam Smith's *Theory of Moral Sentiments*. This is the tradition *The Port Folio* normally has in mind in speaking of "Lord Shaftesbury's opinion, that benevolence is the characteristic of man" (6:1:273); its influence on the terminology of Jefferson's Declaration of Independence has been analyzed by Garry Wills (see *Inventing America*). Yet the great influence on Jefferson's vision of the American republic, as Drew McCoy has persuasively shown, was not the Scottish moral sense theorists but Rousseau, for it is in Rousseau that one discovers not only the doctrine of a natural human innocence, but the idea that this is then subject to warping or distortion by social institutions. This was the context in which, as McCoy puts it, social development would be viewed by Rousseau and Jefferson equally not as improvement but as "a degenerative process that divorced the human soul from its natural qualities of simplicity, goodness, and compassion" (McCoy 24).

The point of calling this doctrine a modern Pelagianism, invoking the original theological controversy between St. Augustine and his antagonist Pelagius, is to acknowledge that the eighteenth-century controversy was also about Original Sin, although no longer as a theological doctrine but as a truth about a human nature perpetually prone to weakness and error. For the original Pelagius had insisted that virtue was obtainable through a simple exercise of the will—this is the sense in which the scheme of moral perfection in Franklin's *Autobiography* makes him so unforgettably the Pelagius of the modern age—against Augustine's equally steady insistence that to make this claim is, wittingly or unwittingly, to tell a great lie about the world. On Augustine's account, the state into which Adam and Eve fell, into which all the generations of their children must be born, is nothing other than the world as mortals actually inhabit it, a world in which, no matter what their resolves or good intentions, people forever find themselves acting in ways that are harmful or weak or self-destructive, bringing evil not only to others but to themselves and those they love.

So far, however, the varieties of modern Pelagianism arising in the eighteenth century might be taken by Federalists as nothing more than a gigantic mistake about human moral nature, a story about innate virtue or innocence the untruth of which is immediately obvious to anyone who, having arisen in the morning determined to overcome temptation and weakness, goes to bed realizing that it has been a day like any other. To men like John Adams and Fisher Ames and Joseph Dennie, the real terror of a widespread Pelagianism, especially dangerous to shallow or unreflective souls because so deeply flattering to their own worst selves, was its further tendency to turn human morality into a matter of mere social convention. For Original Sin, besides being about that part of our moral nature able to recognize itself as prone to weakness and error, had also been about the grounding of human moral values—the "Thou shalt not kill" of God's injunction to Moses and the Israelites—in a divine or transcendent order. To see such rules merely as human conventions, having the same force as a stop sign or a traffic light for a modern driver, was to alter the very conception of social reality.

The shorthand way of putting all this, for Federalists of the *Port Folio* generation, was to say that jacobinism and French revolutionary ideas generally were masks for atheism, which may serve to explain why they were prone to leap so immediately to a charge of atheism when the issues seem under a modern conception to be social or political rather than theological. Thus we hear John Adams already exclaiming in 1790, for instance, at a time when men like Jefferson and Madison were yet wholly enthralled by the French Revolution, that he knew not "what to make of a republic of thirty million atheists" (Hazen 266), and thus a certain thrill goes through the American republic when *The Gazette of the United States* reprints the proud declaration of M. Dupont to the Assembly, on 13 March 1793, that he, at least, is an atheist:

"What! [he exclaims] monarchies are extirpated, thrones are overturned, and scepters are broken to pieces, kings are no more; yet the altars of God remain. Shame to the enlightened spirit of Frenchmen! . . . Nature and reason—these ought to be the gods of man—these are my gods. Kings and priests are leagued in one cursed design—and the cursed instrument of the latter is eternal fire. Let others tremble at this terrific bugbear. As for me, I despise it; as for myself, I here honestly confess to this Assembly I am an atheist. (Hazen 268)

The alternative metaphysics of this French atheism was the materialism of La Mettrie and Helvetius and Holbach, the universe as a purposeless collision of atoms in which mind or consciousness are mere epiphenomena thrown up by a blind whirl of substance. "Let us reason," says the philosophe in a selection from Dr. John Moore's *Mordaunt* reprinted several times in *The Port Folio*. "Were a thousand dice put into a box and thrown out often enough, there can be no doubt but that six thousand [i.e., a thousand sixes] would be thrown out at last; nay, if a hundred thousand were rattled, and thrown without ceasing, six hundred thousand would appear in process of time at one throw. Why, therefore, may not this world, such as we find it, have been cast up by the mere rattling of atoms?" (6:2:185). The universe of the philosophes is one in which religion and revealed truth expose themselves as nothing more than the superstitious reverie of ignorant souls, in which rules or laws regarding murder or theft or adultery seem in some obvious sense products of mere human contrivance, and in which the only gods available to man are, as we have heard M. Dupont say, Nature and Reason.

At the same time, theories of the universe as a blind whirl of substance had existed since antiquity—one need do no more than glance through Lucretius or the surviving fragments of Democritus to divine the ancestry of *Mordaunt*'s philosophe—and held no terrors for Dennie's intellectual circle. The deeper scandal of French revolutionary doctrine was that it then took these as pretexts for a dangerous new idolatry, the golden calf of unaided human reason set up as an actual object of worship for men and women in the modern age. This is that religion of reason the Federalists already hear echoing in the speech of M. Dupont, which they saw as having been given ultimate shape as a modern idolatry in the famous Fête de la Raison in Notre Dame in which the high altar was shrouded, a Temple of Philosophy set up in its stead, and a bare-breasted actress unveiled as the Goddess of Reason to the plaudits of a cheering throng. For *The Port Folio* writers, this would remain the essential tableau of the Revolution, in which "the declaration of atheism and eternal sleep," as one of them remarks, had led by a kind of inevitability to "the transformation of all the churches into temples of reason, the worship of a naked whore, substituted in place of the living God" (1:210).

It is easy enough today to see how the worship or idolatry of reason solved a major problem for Robespierre's party, for when moral law has been exposed as mere convention even revolutionaries will be at a loss for higher principles to justify their actions. The worship of reason, even in the person of an undraped actress or prostitute, is thus a way of announcing that, in a purely material universe, the only remaining source of human values is human consciousness. Yet this was then precisely the move that, for opponents of the French Revolution, abruptly returned the jacobins to a known moral and theological category, for the worship of reason thus viewed is simply humanity's worship of itself. The name of such self-deification is pride, a sin or error as old as the creation. This is what M. Gregoire, formerly the Bishop of Blois and a revolutionary associate of Joel Barlow, tried gently to get across to a Barlow who, in 1808, has still not had his eyes opened about the Revolution. The revolutionaries, reports Gregoire, who to his own sorrow had been there, "exclaimed that no one could be at once a christian and a republican. . . . What would they have substituted for christianity? A goddess, and a temple of reason, man for God himself" (9:2:464).

The notion of self-worship as the primal sin or error, of course, underlies Judeo-Christian moral theology from its beginnings. Yet for anti-jacobin writers in English the great source of imagery for dealing with the primal error was *Paradise Lost*, for Milton's great epic of the war in heaven made clear, in ways that no theological treatise or even the Bible had done, the sense in which rebellion against God is simply the name for a gigantic error of denial or forgetting, a refusal to acknowledge that one's mind or consciousness, on whatever description of the universe one chooses to accept, is not a gift that one has bestowed upon oneself. The fall of Satan and Adam equally, the eighteenth-century theologian William Law had said, was a fall into self, the isolated prison of a separate ego that denies its origins and continuously re-creates the world in the image of its own desires and gratifications. This, to such writers as Burke or Gifford in England or the *Port Folio* writers in America, was precisely to give an account of France in the time of Robespierre and the Terror, and of jacobinism as an abstract body of doctrine invisibly at work elsewhere in modern society.[8]

This again is language that rings strangely in modern ears. The war of Federalism against Jefferson, says Dennie, is nothing less than "a struggle with the baleful powers of hell and democracy." This is the language of *Paradise Lost*, of the fallen angels raising the temple Pandemonium amidst the unearthly flickerings of sulfurous fire, as it will be used by Burke and Fisher Ames and Dennie and scores of lesser writers against the French Revolution, always with the intent of reminding readers that events in France, with sansculottes dancing their bloody bacchanal amidst the flames of revolutionary bonfires, is simply the latest staging of the oldest drama known to God and man. Nor was this a language restricted to believers in the Bible or Christianity. "I begin to fear that Satan will drive me out of possession of Paradise," writes Edward Gibbon, elsewhere the very voice of Enlightenment religious skepticism, in a letter reprinted in *The Port Folio* in 1805. Gibbon is writing to the earl of Sheffield from Switzerland, newly transformed by the victorious armies of the French Revolution into the "Helvetic Republic." "My only comfort will be," he adds gloomily, "that I shall have been expelled by the power and not seduced by the arts of the blackest demon in hell, the demon of democracy" (7:1: 58).

The Port Folio is always careful to register respect for those Americans who, immediately after the storming of the Bastille, had not only been filled with enthusiasm for the French Revolution but had seen it as the natural continuation of their own revolution against England and monarchy. This is the audience towards whom Dennie gestures sympathetically in, for instance, quoting approvingly from a life of Robert Burns written by one Dr. Currie a passage that vividly recaptures the sense of new birth felt on both sides of the Atlantic in the early days of the revolution in France: "Prejudice and tyranny seemed about to disappear from among men, and the day-star of reason to rise upon a benighted world." But then, as even Burns himself had come to realize, untimely called to the grave before events in France had run their fateful course, the day-star had risen over a scene terrible to behold: "In the dawn of this beautiful morning, the genius of French freedom appeared on our southern horizon, with the countenance of an angel, but speedily assumed the features of a demon, and vanished in a shower of blood" (1:410).

For the Federalist writers, the great puzzle is not sympathy with the French Revolution but how such sympathy could be maintained, as Jefferson and his party persisted in doing, even after what Dennie calls "the dark night of jacobinism" (1:150) has set in.[9] Alexander Hamilton will emerge as the symbol of the Federalist order in America, the last great hope of the *Port Folio* writers for a return to the order of civic virtue identified in their minds with Washington and the federal constitution, precisely because he carries into public life so lucid and urgent a sense that the dark secret heart of Jeffersonian democracy, its source in a mysterious malevolence unperceivable by ordinary men and women, has in some crucial way to do with this continued sympathy for a murderous jacobinism. There is tremendous anger, but also an honest perplexity, in the address by Hamilton to the electors of New

York printed in its entirety in *The Port Folio* in 1801. What is it, exactly, Hamilton asks, that the Jeffersonians wish America to perceive in the French Revolution:

> What is there in that terrific picture which you are to admire or imitate? . . . Is it the undistinguishing massacre in prisons and dungeons, of men, women, and children? Is the sanguinary justice of a revolutionary tribunal, or the awful terrors of a guillotine? Is it the rapid succession of revolution upon revolution, erecting the transient power of one set of men upon the tombs of another? Is it the assassinations which have been perpetrated, or the new ones, which are projected? Is it the open profession of impiety in the public assemblies, or the ridiculous worship of a Goddess of Reason? . . . Is it the destruction of commerce, the ruin of manufactures, the oppression of agriculture? . . . If it be none of these things, what is it? (1:162–63)

The reason Jefferson was in no position to renounce the French Revolution has been brilliantly explicated by Joyce Appleby, who demonstrates the manner in which a certain metaphysics of personal autonomy, a vision of individual freedom created by the conditions of an emergent money or market society, were for Jeffersonian ideology the stakes in both the French Revolution and democratic republicanism in America. For Appleby's argument is that the Jeffersonian ascendancy marks the real triumph of Lockean theory, the social contract and liberal individualism, in American politics, and that the French Revolution would for Jefferson himself always symbolize the entry of these principles onto the stage of world history. The *Port Folio* writers entirely agreed, but from a perspective gloomily opposed to Jefferson's progressive optimism. The ideologues of the French Assembly, remarks Dennie at one point, "early entangled themselves with principles, pretended to be drawn from an imaginary state of nature, anterior to civil society," and by doing so "let loose, from every religious or moral restraint, all the most ungovernable passions of the human heart" (1:206).

The great virtue of Appleby's argument taken on its own terms is that it brings so clearly into view the sense in which social contract theory—Hobbes as much as Locke, in her view—is underwritten at an invisible level by an economic or market concept of "contract," the notion of an agreement freely entered into by autonomous and responsible individuals, and then, by implication, the degree to which this entails a certain positive conception of human nature. To see why radical French doctrines of equality remained indispensable to Jeffersonian liberalism even after Robespierre and the rise of Napoleon, in short, is to glimpse the way in which Locke's free individual and Rousseau's innate human innocence had already, some time since, merged in the Jeffersonian idealization of an abstract entity called "the people." This is why, as the Federalist writers intuitively realized, Jefferson's ascendancy signaled the triumph of Pelagian moral doctrine at the public or collective level, the reconsecration of the demos as the sovereign American people. "Democrats suppose themselves, and our nation," remarks one *Port Folio* writer somewhat sourly, "to be in a sinless state, from which they cannot fall" (3:137).

The great virtue of Appleby's argument for an understanding of literary Federalism, on the other hand, is that it makes clear why Dennie and the *Port Folio* writers are so unremitting in their identification of Jefferson and his party with a money or market society, and why they persist in portraying Jeffersonian America as a land of "soul destroying dollars," in Cobbett's telling phrase (*A Year's Residence* 407), in which they saw the ceaseless pursuit of material interest as decomposing society into a mere aggregate of isolated individuals. The America of Jeffersonian liberalism appears in *The Port Folio* as a place where, as in France, abstract doctrines and visionary schemes are destroying genuine community—there is in Jeffersonian America no "speculation that John Locke or Algernon Sidney has hazarded respecting Civil Liberty and Natural Rights," snorts Dennie, "but appears in the shape of a mathematical demonstration" (6:2:250)—but where the consequence is a slower, more silent revolution in which a new world of Hobbesian or Mandevillian egoism has learned to pass itself off under doctrines of "freedom" and "autonomy," and where a society entirely given over to material striving has been taught to celebrate itself, amidst its tabloid newspapers and spittoons, as the very pinnacle of modern civilization.

To Federalist writers able to perceive in his America nothing more than naked self- interest and slow moral deterioration, Jefferson thus comes to seem the great mystifier of the new rule of the demos, less a political leader than a propagandist attempting to dress an unlovely social reality in one or another doctrine of natural innocence. This is why, to such Federalists as Fisher Ames, the most egregious of Jefferson's mystifications has to do with his pose as a classical republican of Country party lineage, what Ames once calls his "monstrous affectation of pure republicanism, primitive simplicity, and extraordinary zeal for the public good." For this was the pose, as Ames and the *Port Folio* writers saw it, that had permitted Jefferson illegitimately to mobilize against Federalism an idiom of luxury and commerce and cor-

15

ruption, to awaken sleeping memories of Robert Walpole and the South Sea Bubble—"to cry down the funding system," as Ames somewhat testily says, "the Bank, and the Excise Law, as emanations from the Secretary of the Treasury; to endeavor to make those measures odious to the people and then attribute them all to Mr. H[amilton]'s machinations" (*Works* 973).

The spirit in which *The Port Folio* enters into its campaign against Jefferson and such spokesmen for his ideology as Duane and *The Aurora*, what Dennie once calls "the major and minor scribblers of democracy" (3:215), is thus one of struggle against an entire order of unreality, a world of systematic illusion and a nation inexplicably electing to honor the illusion rather than the reality. *The Port Folio*'s sense of its own role in Jeffersonian America is nowhere better caught, perhaps, than in the prospectus of a Baltimore paper printed by Dennie as an eloquent restatement of his own objectives as a Federalist editor. The Jeffersonian ascendancy, says this prospectus, marks the rise to power of men "who, under the cloak of false patriotism, of affected adoration of the people . . . like wolves in sheep's clothing endeavor to gain entrance into the fold, and to devour the flock." The great and worthy objective of Federalist writing is thus to dispel illusion, "to present democracy in its native deformity, by stripping off its assumed mask of republicanism: to rescue that . . . venerated name, from the disgrace which it must otherwise suffer, by its forced and unnatural association with democracy" (2:30).

To Dennie and the *Port Folio* writers, the preeminent example of a mystified society, an order of the basest self-interest hiding behind the noblest protestations of liberty and equality, was the slave owning South in general and, in particular, the Virginia of Jefferson, Madison, and Monroe. For in the Virginia of the great slave owning plantations, in a class of wealthy landowners professing a vocal and unwavering sympathy with revolutionary France, *The Port Folio* saw a society in which nothing was as it seemed, a world of unreality with its inhabitants so taken in by their own rhetoric that they dwelt as though in a delusion or a dream. This is the context in which the familiar themes of anti-Jeffersonian polemic in *The Port Folio*—attacks on slavery as an institution, assaults on the three-fifths rule giving slave owners representation in Congress for Negroes owned as property, hints of a growing sectional antipathy between New England and the South— must always be taken as the most urgent of warnings about mystification as such, a world in which the national existence threatens to become as delusional as it already is in Jefferson's Virginia.

This is not to say that *The Port Folio*'s detestation of slavery, its ceaseless protestations that blacks and whites are equally human and therefore equally entitled to justice, is not just what it seems, the origin in the Federalism of writers like Dennie and Fisher Ames and Josiah Quincy of that New England abolitionism that would so inexorably lead to the Emancipation Proclamation. There are in *The Port Folio* scores of pointed anecdotes like the one in which a slave owner, discussing the Negro problem in a regionally mixed company, is driven at last to seek consensus on the one principle he takes to be uncontroversial: "You will allow, I hope, that they are an inferior race of men?" And *The Port Folio*'s answer is always that of the gentleman present who, given the massive reality of slavery as an institution, can only seek refuge in a wry irony: "I will allow that their hair is short and ours long, . . . that their skin is black and ours white; yet after all these concessions, I still have my doubts respecting our rights to make them slaves" (7:1:103).

Nonetheless, the ultimate intolerability is the spectacle of a slave owning society whose spokesmen never cease praising revolutionary France and who just as unremittingly accuse their Federalist opponents of being aristocratic by temperament, monarchial in their political sympathies and, worst of all, partisans of England in its war against Napoleon. "They say," observes one *Port Folio* writer impatiently, "there is a British faction, an aristocratic and monarchial party in America" (1:154), and the ideologues of Jeffersonian democracy would reiterate the charge as though all the while unaware that Jefferson, himself a Virginia slave owner, might be viewed as representing something resembling an aristocratic order, what Fisher Ames once calls a class of "lazy feudal barons" (*Works* 313). This is a point about Virginia that *The Port Folio* will strive again and again to bring to light. "The political power of the state," notes one writer almost plaintively, ". . . is in the hands of the great landholders, the men of thousands of acres, who, in effect, are the possessors of lordships" (1:399).

For *The Port Folio*, the point of such sobering reminders is never simply to discredit Jefferson personally. It is to insist that the republicanism of the Southern democrats, claiming roots in Country ideology and speaking a Lockean language of natural rights and individual freedom, may be seen as a grand order of mystification meant ultimately to re-create the nation in its own image. Thus, for instance, a satiric sketch such as *Virginia Patriotism*, in which the planter Fraternal rehearses the "extemporary" speech he means to give at next week's county meeting, is not simply about southern political hypocrisy but an America that, given the tremendous attractions of Jeffersonian mystification, might very well someday find itself governed on just the same terms:

Fraternal: . . . Oh, divine, solacing, beneficent, convenient Spirit of freedom, it is thou that producest these desirable effects! We are all free, we are all equal. Thy great modern apostle, the illustrious, the wonderful, the never to be forgotten Jefferson, has clearly proved that this is a self-evident truth—All men have an unalienable right to"—(here a black enters, and accidentally stumbling, strikes the extended arm of the patriotical speaker, and knocks the paper from his hand—which last kicks and beats him most unmercifully.) O you idle, impertinent, blundering scoundrel—to break in upon one thus, when I had arrived at the most interesting, eloquent, and pathetic part of my speech, at the very instant when I was going to demonstrate the equality of all men, of what rank, station, and talents soever! to be interrupted in this manner! 'Tis insufferable; (still kicks and beats him) villain, you shall be tied up and well whipped for this." (3:245)

This is the context in which *The Port Folio*'s treatment of the Sally Hemings affair, in which Jefferson's rumored sexual relations with a slave mistress would become a favorite topic of Federalist satire, demands to be understood less as a personal attack than as a symbolic episode having to do with southern culture as a world of illusion or mystification. For the puzzle of the Hemings episode has always been that writers who in every other instance considered themselves to be above mere personal vilification so evidently saw nothing wrong with satirizing Jefferson's supposed relations with Sally. Thus Thomas Moore, for instance, already solidly established as a rising younger poet in England, is wholly unembarrassed about memorializing his visit to Jeffersonian America with a poem in which Jefferson, returning from freedom's councils, retires at the end of the day to "dream of freedom in his bondmaid's arms." And thus John Quincy Adams, stern in his moral attitudes and classical in his literary taste, can turn an odd moment to adapting Horace's ode to the slave girl Xanthia Phoceus to Jefferson and Sally ("Dear Thomas, deem it no disgrace/With slaves to mend thy breed" [1:302]).[10]

The symbolic overtones of the Hemings episode arise partly from the irony, obvious from the large number of mulatto children in the southern states, that planters are willing enough to grant their slaves equality at the level of sexual attraction. Black males, Jefferson had notoriously said in his *Notes on the State of Virginia*, always show a sexual preference for white women, just as the orang-outang prefers black women to females of its own species. *The Port Folio* mounts a number of satiric attacks on the crude proto-Darwinism of this analogy, in which blacks in effect become the missing link between the higher primates and a superior white creation, but its strongest sarcasm is reserved for the assertion that there is only a one-way sexual attraction between blacks and whites. To the contrary, says one *Port Folio* writer, there are more than enough mixed-race children in evidence to "testify that the regard is mutual" and that some white males, at least, "do not feel the abhorrence which they might naturally be expected to have," on Jefferson's argument, for blacks as an inferior "set of beings" (4:251).

Beyond the logic of natural or biological equality so undeniable whenever the child of a white slave owner is born to a black mother, the *Port Folio* writers always see another satiric subtext in the Sally Hemings affair. This is the three-fifths rule giving southerners increased congressional representation in proportion to their slaves.[11] "In a state where a slavery of man is established by law," observed the Massachusetts legislature in a resolution prominently reprinted in *The Port Folio*, "the slaves have no voice in the elections—but a Planter, possessing fifty slaves, may be considered as having thirty votes, while a farmer in Massachusetts . . . is confined to a single vote" (4:261). So, as in the bitterly satiric verses of Thomas Green Fessenden's *Democracy Unveiled*, a slave owner begetting children is actually increasing his representation in Congress:

> Great men can never lack supporters,
> Who manufacture their own voters;
> Besides 'tis plain as yonder steeple,
> They will be fathers to the people. (II, 35)

The point of the Sally Hemings episode thus has to do with a political culture based on illusion and empty rhetoric, and the mystery dwelt upon by *The Port Folio* is how Jefferson, as the representative of such a culture, can be taken by so many Americans as the very symbol of a new and attractive democratic order.

At a certain point in its campaign against Jefferson, however, *The Port Folio* begins to realize that no amount of moral outrage directed at slavery or the Virginia oligarchy is going to make any impression on an American populace mesmerized by the rhetoric of Jeffersonian democracy, that Jefferson and his party have somehow synthesized out of various materials—Country party ideology, Lockean individualism, French revolutionary principles—a language of natural equality and virtue so powerful as to neutralize any competing vision of the American republic. The genius of Jeffersonian democracy has been its power to convince Americans that they actually inhabit the fantasy of natural innocence contained in works like Crevecoeur's *Letters from an American Farmer*. "All the European nations," says Dietrich von Bulow, a German traveler whose letters were reprinted serially in *The Port Folio*, ". . . complain of an unusual degree of immorality; they do not give themselves out as virtuous; whereas the Americans say of themselves that they are a people of simple manners, far exalted above the corruption of Europe: that among them still reigns the patriarchal happiness of the golden age" (2:226).

The Port Folio grasps as well that the tremendous popular appeal of Jeffersonian democracy has somehow to do with its idealization of agriculture. In the neo-Harringtonian language of Country ideology, in which the landowning nobility and gentry of England had been viewed as what Pocock calls its community of virtue, land had been a symbol of the community in its permanent aspect, the nation that is always there as generations pass away. This was the symbolic import that Federalism saw as losing its intelligibility in an America where land was limitlessly and indiscriminately available to all classes, which, to writers like Dennie and Fisher Ames, is what had explained and justified Hamilton's attempt to develop a new kind of property in the nation through an integrated vision of commerce, credit, and agriculture. The effect, as Federalists would realize only belatedly, was to leave Jeffersonian ideology in sole possession of an ancient language of agrarian virtue, the locus classicus of which is Jefferson's famous remarks on agriculture in *Notes on the State of Virginia*:

> Those who labour in the earth are the chosen people of God, if ever he had a chosen people, whose breasts he has made his peculiar deposit for substantial and genuine virtue. It is the focus in which he keeps alive that sacred fire, which otherwise might escape from the face of the earth. Corruption of morals in the mass of cultivators is a phenomenon of which no age nor nation has furnished an example. . . . Generally speaking, the proportion which the aggregate of the other classes of citizens bears in any state to that of its husbandmen, is the proportion of its unsound to its healthy parts, and is a good-enough barometer whereby to measure its degree of corruption.[12]

The initial response of *The Port Folio* is to deny that the mere ownership of land has power to bestow automatic virtue upon its possessor, to try to demonstrate that Jefferson's vision of agrarian innocence is really a disguised Pelagianism invisibly and illegitimately drawing its authority from a conception of civic virtue to which it is fundamentally opposed, the classical republican ideal of georgic labor in which it is the industry and piety of the husbandman, and not the simple ownership of arable acres, that maintains the polity in prosperity and peace.[13] In a Jeffersonian democracy driven by the pursuit of material gain, the georgic virtues are precisely the first to vanish. "The commercial character," says the geographer Dr. Aiken, whose writings Dennie continuously holds up in *The Port Folio* as a mirror to his countrymen, "seems radical in the Americans. Agriculture is pursued on a trading principle; and nothing is more common than, when a new seller has . . . cleared a spot, and brought it into a tolerable state of cultivation, that he disposes of it on profitable terms, and recommences his toils in the solitary forest" (6:1:311).

Already in Aiken's observations there is visible an America in which land is to become simply one commodity among others and where vast ventures in land speculation will be masked or mystified in a Jeffersonian language of agrarian innocence, of an independent yeomanry spreading out across the trackless wilderness carrying with it the virtues of democratic republicanism. To many Federalists such language seemed too transparent to succeed even with a demos wishing eagerly to be deceived. "However land-jobbers may try to prolong their credit by painting Kentucky and Tennessee as a new Arcadia," grumbled Fisher Ames in 1801, "the evidence of facts will prevail" (*Works* 210). Yet such commentators as Ames had not reckoned with the tremendous market energies already visible to a traveler like Bulow in the 1790s: "the richest of the Americans are not those, who possess the largest cultivated farms; they are those . . . who circulate the most paper. . . . In a word, the speculators, especially in lands, compose this class" (2:171).

The notion of speculation or land-jobbing as the demystified truth of Jeffersonian democracy explains the prominence given in *The Port Folio* to Bulow's *Travels in America*, translated from the German by John Quincy Adams and appearing in serialized form throughout most of 1802. For Bulow's image of an America driven entirely by avarice and greed and low commercial dishonesty, sinking into ignorance and squalor even while boasting vaingloriously of its republican virtue, was so unflattering as to draw protests even from Federalist readers. Dennie's response, made with no attempt to defend every detail of Bulow's account, was simply to suggest that an America that had just voted Jefferson into the presidency had something to learn from the way it was viewed by travelers from other nations. A thousand details in Bulow's *Travels* contribute to the counterimage Dennie holds up to Jeffersonian America, but the theme that predominates is land speculation:

A tax upon uncultivated lands would have . . . promoted the general welfare. . . . The speculators, then, would have been obliged to sell their deserts, cheap and at once, in small portions to the poor, who would have cultivated them. But now, having nothing to pay for their extensive tracts of land, they can wait their own time. . . . Hence it is very difficult for the poor to obtain land cheap, in a part of the world, where such extensive ranges of woods only wait for the hand of the laborious planter, to be transformed from gloomy wilds into smiling fields, adorned with golden harvests. Hence the dispersed situation of the inhabitants on the boundaries, which dooms them to poverty beyond description . . . for they push forward to the inmost parts of the forest, in order there to clear some land, unknown to the proprietor, from whom they can purchase none. . . . But the fault is in the people themselves, inasmuch as every one, who has money, prefers speculation to farming. These land-speculators create a very pernicious uncertainty and insecurity of property; for . . . land may pass, perhaps, through the hands of ten speculators in one day. (2:172)

To the Jeffersonian fable of agrarian innocence, *The Port Folio* thus counterposes an image of America as a country in which a frenzy of land speculation is undermining every remaining vestige of honor or probity, where the way to wealth lies not in productive toil but in cheating Indians of their ancestral hunting grounds and selling spurious claims to unsuspecting foreigners. "The frauds of the land speculators are well known," says Bulow, "especially as there is in Germany no scarcity of sufferers by such deceptions. . . . Naked rocks are sold for good land, and false maps of them exhibited to foreigners. The Indians are shamefully cheated out of their lands; for they are first made drunk, and then their lands are bought of them" (2:227).[14] "A great many anecdotes . . . are remembered of our fraudulent sales of land," echoes an American writing to *The Port Folio* from France nearly ten years later, "of families prevailed upon to quit Paris in the hope of plenty upon easy terms in some happier region, who have afterwards found themselves exposed to all the bitterness of want in unwholesome climates" (10:1:196).

For the Federalist writers, the effect of such testimony is to explain Jefferson's association with such personages as Joel Barlow, a propagandist of French radical ideas grown immensely rich by promoting American land schemes in Europe, or "citizen Tench Coxe," as *The Port Folio* once calls him, the enormous scale of whose land speculations could be taken to account for his desertion to the Jeffersonian party. Yet in literary or cultural terms, its effect is to establish a countermyth to the America of Crevecoeur or Jefferson's *Notes on the State of Virginia*, to bring relentlessly to light a nation whose real image is to be discovered in Franklin's *Way to Wealth* and whose protestations of republican simplicity are a transparent mask for naked self-interest. "Such romantic works as 'The American Farmer's Letters' . . . ," says the poet Tom Moore, "would seduce us into a belief, that innocence, peace, and freedom had deserted the rest of the world for Martha's Vineyard and the banks of the Ohio. . . . A visit to the country is, however, quite sufficient to correct even the most enthusiastic prepossession" (6:2:152–53).

For Dennie and the *Port Folio* writers, land speculation thus becomes the grand metaphor for a money or market society unrecognized as such by its own deluded citizenry, an atomized aggregation of separate or isolated individuals rapidly losing touch with any larger vision of community. "The inhabitants of Kentucky and Tennessee," muses one of *The Port Folio*'s political writers, "have very little attachment to their eastern brethren. Their interests are totally separate. . . . Not one of them, who are arrived at years of maturity, was born upon the spot. They are . . . all speculators or agricultural adventurers . . . who have no more idea of national honor and independence, who think no more about their ancestors, or their posterity, than the gamblers of Change Alley" (2:255). This is Jefferson's supposedly noble yeomanry seen from a Federalist viewpoint, a new world of private interest and individual self-aggrandizement as it appears when seen from the perspective of the classical republican vision of organic society.

As the above writer's mention of Kentucky and Tennessee suggests, the specter of the demos in its Jeffersonian guise is embodied, in Federalist writing, in the person of the backwoodsman, the very image of the separate or isolated individual who, unwilling to dwell within the complex network of mutual rights and responsibilities that constitutes genuine community, has renounced its claims and gone to live amidst the squalor of bare subsistence on the margins of society. "In the hinderparts of Georgia," says a *Port Folio* writer in 1803, "we are told that there is a rude and ferocious horde of ruffians, with all the sturdy vices of the savage, and not one of his virtues" (3:207). In modern ears, once again, to which Jeffersonian democratic ideology has been transmitted as a certain mythology of log-cabin democracy and the common man, any impatience with the rudeness of life on the frontier rings strangely. Yet in the literary moment of *The Port Folio*, whose writers saw themselves as resisting the growing hegemony of just this ideology, it seemed an impatience only with mystification.

To see why the American backwoodsman seemed in Federalist eyes the personification of the Jeffersonian demos at its worst, it is necessary to grasp the opposing vision of community implied by Fisher Ames's enumeration of Federalism's natural constituency as "the householders, tradesmen, and yeomanry of the nation" (*Works* 245). And to grasp this vision of community, which for New England Federalists like Ames and Dennie was not a vision but simply the lived reality of existence in the towns and villages of their own New England,[15] one must today read nearly forgotten works such as Timothy Dwight's *Travels* or *Greenfield Hill*, taking with absolute moral seriousness their world of farmsteads and well-tilled fields and village schools and libraries, of roads and bridges voluntarily built and maintained by the community, a world where usage or custom are tacit ways of honoring the labor and wisdom of one's ancestors and where one's own labors for a posterity one will never live to see are a way of honoring an otherwise invisible ideal of community.[16] For Federalism, this is the world whose claims are renounced by those rootless souls who flee the eastern seaboard for the back country.

In the early years of *The Port Folio*, the Jeffersonian demos may be already glimpsed in Bulow's descriptions of the backwoods settlements or in still-recent memories of the Whiskey Rebellion. Yet as the years of Jefferson's presidency pass away, as celebrations of America as a land of republican simplicity and pastoral innocence are more and more taken by the great mass of its population as the truth about themselves, and as the dwindling voice of Federalism is made out to be the mere muttering of a "monied interest" or "aristocratical party," the demos looms larger and larger in the pages of the magazine, until one realizes that it has, in effect, become America. By 1810 one may open *The Port Folio* to find a long account by Alexander Wilson, author of *The American Ornithologist*, of a journey down the Ohio River:

> The inhabitants of these forlorn sheds will talk to you with pride of the richness of their soil, of the excellence and abundance of their country, of the healthiness of their climate, and the purity of their waters, while the only bread you find among them is of Indian corn coarsely ground. . . . Even their cattle are destitute of stables and hay, and look like moving skeletons; their own houses worse than pig styes; their clothes an assemblage of rags, their faces yellow, and lank with disease. . . . All this is the effect of laziness. The corn is thrown into the ground in the spring, and the pigs turned into the woods, where they multiply like rabbits.

The labor of the squatter is now over till fall, and he spends the winter in eating pork, cabbage and hoe-cakes. (10:1:505–6)

To the very end of their warfare against Jeffersonian democracy, however, Dennie and the *Port Folio* writers never really understand that they have lost the battle because, in surrendering to Jefferson and his party a symbolism of agrarian virtue associated with their own tradition of classical republican values, they have left themselves marooned or isolated without a language with which to combat the forces of an emergent money or market society. Jefferson's embrace of the classical republican equation between landed status and civic virtue, and the daring move of then claiming America's seemingly limitless acres as an unlimited source of such civic virtue,[17] would underwrite a symbolism so powerful as actually to become the American ideology. The lank and sickly settlers of Alexander Wilson's journey down the Ohio are visible on such terms for virtually the last time in the pages of *The Port Folio* under Dennie's editorship. Within a few short years they will have vanished to reappear as the common man of Jacksonian democracy, the independent frontiersman of Frederick Jackson Turner, and the sovereign people of American civic mythology, all tracing their ideological ancestry to the virtuous yeomanry of Jefferson's *Notes on the State of Virginia*.

In the same way, the *Port Folio* writers would never altogether grasp the way in which the symbolism of agrarian virtue had permitted Jeffersonian democracy to define itself in opposition to a shadowy "monied interest," mobilizing a Country party vocabulary of luxury and corruption against an imaginary conspiracy of speculators and power-brokers and would-be aristocrats, thus perpetuating as an internalized dynamic of American national ideology the principle of French revolutionary thought in which the interests of the sovereign people are always seen as being directly opposed to those of what radicals like Joel Barlow denounced as "the privileged orders." In vain would *The Port Folio* protest that the slave owning oligarchy of Jefferson's Virginia was America's closest approximation to a European aristocracy, or that land speculation on the scale practiced by Barlow or "citizen Tench Coxe" was an infinitely greater source of civic corruption than anything known in Walpolian England.

The literary Federalists of the *Port Folio* generation did come to understand, however, that Jeffersonian democracy as they opposed it was something without historical precedent, not an appeal to the demos on the model of Pisistratus in Athens or the Gracchi in ancient Rome but, in effect, a machine of ideological mystification so powerful as actually to be producing a demos, an ever-expanding population of souls driven by the endless pursuit of material gain, where none had existed before. "Are not our people wholly engrossed by the pursuit of wealth and pleasure?" asks Fisher Ames at the beginning of Jefferson's second term. "Though grouped together into a society, the propensities of the individual still prevail" (*Works* 156). "Money has become the god of our idolatry," says a writer in *The Port Folio* at about the same time, "and every noble passion of the soul is lost in it. That high-minded patriotism, which gives dignity to our nature, and character to our country . . . [is] almost smothered and extinguished under heaps of ill-gotten gold, and reams of fraudulent paper" (7:2:28).

These are the terms in which, as Napoleon gradually imposes his will on the French nation and the terror of jacobinism proportionately recedes from Federalist consciousness, *The Port Folio* begins to understand that the demon of democracy in its American guise will be that of a money or market society whose powers of social transformation are so great as to leave nothing, men or women or institutions or the very landscape, unchanged. The radicalism of the French Revolution thus begins to reappear in the America of *The Port Folio* as the longer, slower revolution of economic individualism, a revolution not of guillotines and midnight hangings but of mass markets and mass tastes, a machinery of numerical democracy in which "the tyranny of the many," as Fisher Ames once calls it—"the unlearned reason of a majority," as Dennie more impatiently puts it, "told by the head"—will eventually be made to seem instead a noble experiment in democratic self-governance.

In the early years of *The Port Folio*, the warfare against Jeffersonian democracy is carried on almost wholly in political terms, in the name of a classical republican vision the Federalist writers identify with America in the period of Washington's governance. This is the happy republican system so earnestly recommended to the regard of his grand jurors by Judge Addison, what we have heard Alexander Hamilton describe to the electors of New York as the mild reign of rational liberty, the well-balanced government of Aristotelian or Polybian theory as it preserves the peace and prosperity of all its citizens. Only in the years of Jefferson's second term, as the demonic visage of modern democracy begins more and more to appear as the indiscriminate populism of a mass market society, do the terms of Federalist opposition shift gradually from the political to the cultural, becoming instead a prolonged protest against the cost to mind or spirit exacted by a society whose only values are those of economic individualism. This is the moment at which literary Federalism, born in the ferment of opposition to Jeffersonian democracy and only gradually accepting the inevitability of what I shall call its retreat from history, becomes the first serious exploration in American writing of "the consequence," in Quentin Anderson's memorable phrase, "of living in a society imaginatively dominated by money and the process of exchange" ("Cultural Office" 206). In the pages of *The Port Folio*, this will emerge initially as an anxiety about the fate of literature in a democracy, a worry that in the new age of the common man there will not only be no books and readers, but not even the memory of a time when a shared acquaintance with Homer and Virgil and Shakespeare could be taken as an invisible principle of community. Literature in America languishes in obscurity, laments Dennie in 1807, "because men leave in cold neglect every liberal pursuit; because Avarice is the tutelary power of the country" (7:2:342). Only gradually would it dawn on Dennie and the *Port Folio* writers that such laments as this belong themselves to an established literary tradition, raising the unexpected possibility that it might be permitted to Federalism, though doomed to vanish from the sphere of American politics, to survive instead as a mode of American writing.

Chapter Two

Oliver Oldschool

THROUGHOUT the eight years of its publication as a weekly periodical, and then for several more during its continuation as a monthly, *The Port Folio* carried on its masthead the name not of Joseph Dennie but of one Oliver Oldschool, Esq. In using Oldschool as an imaginary editorial persona, Dennie was observing a literary convention originating in mid-eighteenth-century London with Edward Cave, who had created the imaginary editor Sylvanus Urban to impose unity of outlook on *The Gentleman's Magazine*, the first modern periodical to contain a variety of contributors and departments. This remains the point when Oliver Oldschool presides as an imaginary presence over *The Port Folio*: "Although you are not the writer of all that appears in your paper," remarks one of Oldschool's correspondents, "yet, are you supposed to sanction, by your approbation, the sentiments offered to the public, through that medium" (1:123). In addition, Dennie intended Oliver Oldschool's name to signal his own lifelong idealization of Oliver Goldsmith, and thus the allegiance of *The Port Folio* to Augustan standards in literature and politics.

The Goldsmith who presides as a symbolic presence over *The Port Folio* is the Goldsmith of such works as *The Deserted Village* and *The Vicar of Wakefield*, whose genius had been to catch an older traditional or organic community at the very moment of its vanishing. Even in Dennie's earlier *Lay Preacher* essays, whose imaginary persona was more directly inspired by Laurence Sterne's Parson Yorick, this Goldsmith is felt as a continuous influence. For the original *Lay Preachers*, as Dennie will recall when the series is subsequently resumed in *The Port Folio*, had been written in Walpole, New Hampshire, "in a village retirement, among a frank and honest people, of primeval principles and uniform conduct"—a world, in short, meant specifically to recall the older England of hedgerow and hamlet and immemorial custom preserved in Goldsmith's writings. "All my adventures," says the Lay Preacher about that earlier setting, "like those of the vicar of Wakefield, were by the fire side" (4:158). This is the world of peace and order that reappears in *The Port Folio* whenever the magazine reprints one of the earlier *Lay Preacher* essays, which thus come to serve as a measure of the deterioration of American life under Jefferson. It is also a world assumed to be on its way to moral extinction.

For Federalists, as we have seen, the threat of extinction is posed by those French revolutionary doctrines that in America have rematerialized in the guise of Jeffersonian democracy, underlying which is the self-flattering Pelagian assumption of an innate human virtue or innocence. The philosophers of the modern age, the great Federalist spokesman Timothy Dwight had witheringly said in a much-discussed sermon, thinking of Frenchmen like Rousseau and Condorcet and Americans like Franklin and Jefferson, "have discovered, that men are naturally wise and good, prone to submit to good government, and pleased to have their passions and appetites restrained; and that all the errors and iniquities of our species are derived merely from the oppression of the privileged and the great" (*Sermons* 1:303). Such Federalists as Dwight and Dennie thought that one need look no farther for the doctrine that in France had produced Robespierre and the Terror, mass murders and hangings and the guillotine, and in America the noisy celebrations of Genet and Liberty, the declamations of jacobin clubs and democratic societies, and now the political ascendancy of Jefferson and a new backwoods democracy proclaiming the ragged frontier settler the very avatar of the common man.

This is a lesson that one actually sees Dennie learning over the period that he is writing *The Lay Preacher*. For in the original series of *Lay Preacher* essays it had been the din of the French Revolution, and of celebration in the democratic societies of America, that awakened the Preacher from his dream of republican simplicity, taught him the fateful lesson that a community in which men and women act virtuously is only to be won through a collective struggle against human weakness and selfishness and pride, that the New England village life he had been taking for granted was really the precarious gift of an ancestral wisdom that, having managed after long trial to make honesty and decency habitual, had passed the habit along to its posterity. This is the unhappy truth that pulls *The Lay Preacher* more and more towards the maelstrom of events occurring in the outside world, until the later essays enter into a full engagement with jacobinism in France and democratic republicanism in America:

In a lawless and capricious Commonwealth, all the powers of anarchy, madness, absurdity, and malevolence delight to dwell.

29

Men agree in nothing, except to perpetuate delusion, and to sanctify folly. . . . They hate and persecute each other, with all the malice and vindictiveness of Republicanism. Having renounced all sobriety of intellect—having shut their eyes to the broad blaze of the steady lights of Experience—having stopped their ears to exclude the warning voice of eternal Wisdom, they rush forward, and with the savage fury of Milton's fiend, "Arm'd with hell flames and fury all at once/O'er heaven's high towers to force resistless way." (5:242)

The name Oliver Oldschool is meant to announce that *The Port Folio* will speak from a moral perspective in which the memory of a coherent past always provides the basis for a critique of modernity. This is the reason that the Federalist writers are always able so spontaneously to use the idiom of classical republicanism in identifying Jeffersonian democracy as a form of corruption and decline. "Had our people been what they were in '76," says a writer in *The Port Folio*'s "Politics" department in 1804, "Jefferson would not have been president in 1801. Were they now what they were in '89, he could not be president in 1805. The people are changed" (4:235). The spirit of jacobinism in America, says another writer, is only to be resisted "by the old habits, and manners, and morals, of our country" (3:137). *The Port Folio*, says Dennie himself, speaking as Oliver Oldschool at a time when hopes for a reversal of Jeffersonian democracy are still high, is addressed to "the sound portion of the American community," "the ANCIENT GENTLEMEN" whose "old fashioned principles" must be expected eventually to prevail (1:262).

Literary Federalism as it emerges under the aegis of Oliver Oldschool during Jefferson's presidency thus begins in an attempt to understand recent history in classical republican terms. For the Federalist writers would always view the American republic as it had emerged from the Revolutionary War as having been primarily a recovery of civic virtue within the English constitutional tradition. On these terms, the emergence of jacobinism and Jeffersonian democracy can only be understood as corruption crying out for return to a republic that had existed just yesterday. "The people are changed," we have heard one *Port Folio* writer cry.[1] At the time of the Revolution, "the continent seemed animated with one genius, pure and honorable." Now all is altered:

There is reason more and more to apprehend that the moral principle of society is relaxed and tainted to the core; and that it is in the growing corruption of our national character that democracy, laboring still to increase that corruption, now feels her strength and hopes to preserve it. Or rather we might say she hopes and feels this not only in the corruption of our national character, but in its loss and total oblivion. Once, in the struggles of our revolution, at the eras of the congress of independence, of the convention at Philadelphia, . . . in those times we had a national character. It was a character for wisdom and integrity, for sober discernment, for constancy, for gratitude, for public spirit, for the glow and vigilance of rational liberty, and stubbornness and tenacity of right, for decent and temperate, and legal and solemn restraints, if not for the seriousness of hallowed piety and religious devotion. . . . Our republic appeared abroad to be once more realizing on earth the fables and dreams of history, or exemplifying its truths in an emulation and rivalship of Grecian and Roman worth. (4:235)

This is the classical republican diagnosis of corruption and decline as the source of present evil, with "corruption"—always in this civic language the gloomy opposite of "virtue"—implying a dissolution of society into atomistic egoism, a world of individuals driven entirely by self-gratification in which no one any longer lives for the good of the community as a whole. In earlier classical republican thinking, Country party ideology in England and America or literary Augustanism in its long warfare against Walpole and the Robinocracy, the source of corruption had always been Luxury, the too-great material prosperity that, in the cyclical theory of history, signals the beginning of the end of a nation's greatness. By the time *The Port Folio* is moved to undertake its opposition to Jeffersonian democracy, the Federalist writers will have begun to see the enemy as a market society as such: the "spirit of honor, which animated every bosom of every citizen of the ancient Republics . . . cannot exist in a country where traffic is the only employment that commands attention, and gold the only attribute that gives rank and consequence. . . . Love of country is lost, absorbed, sunk in the love of self" (7:2:29).[2]

From our own perspective, taking Jeffersonian democracy as the ideology of an emergent money or market society seems in some obvious sense to mean that one must come to grips with new and impersonal forces of social transformation wholly unknown in the world of the ancient republics, and that therefore have no place in classical republican thought. But this was not true for the Federalist writers, for reasons that will turn out to be crucial to the development of literary Federalism. For the deep continuity of human history is guaranteed, on a Federalist interpretation, by a human moral nature that remains perpetually the same beneath the vicissitudes of historical change. This is what reduces to mere technicality all questions about the precise difference between ancient luxury and modern economic individualism. What remains true about democracy, in ancient Athens or modern Paris, is that it represents the war of human pride against all restraint. "The natural vanity, presumption, and restlessness of the human heart have," said Fisher Ames, "from the first, afforded the strength of a host to the jacobins in our country" (*Works* 161). The deeper truth of classical republican theory, in short, has for the Federalists always lain in its vision of corruption as an egoism or naked self-interest that threatens to destroy community. This is a truth that survives whether expressed as the luxury of the ancient republics or economic self-interest in Jeffersonian America.

The Port Folio counterposes to this specter of corruption, here not needing to diverge in the slightest from classical republicanism orthodoxy, a vision of civic virtue as disinterestedness or unselfish commitment to the community as a whole. The archaic origins of this vision, as Linda Dowling has shown, lie in a warrior ethos in which the great archetype of civic virtue is the willingness of the citizen-soldier, Greek hoplite or Roman legionary, to give his life in the name of a community not present on the field of battle, to die that the polis might live.[3] This is the archetype Dennie has in mind when he speaks of "the *virtus*, or military fortitude of the Romans" (9:1:455), and it is the half-mythic ideal, associated with the images of Leonidas and Cincinnatus and the Horatii, that *The Port Folio* always means to invoke in reminding readers that Washington and Hamilton, the heroes of its Federalism, had also been heroes of the Revolutionary War.

The same notion of *virtus*, the warrior or hero as the very embodiment of the community in his willingness to die for the polis, carries over to the idea of the virtuous magistrate as guardian of the republic in peace. Thus Federalism will see a species of martial heroism, for instance, in Washington's determination to maintain American neutrality at a time when tremendous pressure was coming from "democratic republicans" to enter the conflict between France and England on the side of revolutionary France. "He stood," Fisher Ames would write later, "like Leonidas at the pass at Thermopylae, to defend our independence": "Time was gained for the citizens to recover their virtue and good sense, and they soon recovered them. The crisis was passed, and America was saved" (*Works* 535). The same sort of military metaphors as they occur in *The Port Folio* are meant to remind readers that the warfare through which the republic is preserved, while sometimes against external enemies, is always at the same time against human presumption at home.

The last great expression of this notion of virtue in classical antiquity had come in the speeches and writings of Cicero during the dissolution of the Roman republic. This is why the voice of Cicero is so often heard in the pages of *The Port Folio* during the early years when the Federalists are still thinking of the Jeffersonian ascendancy as a temporary aberration, and why Cicero's discussions of civic virtue are taken by Federalists as implicit idealizations of George Washington. Like those appointed as the legal guardians of an orphan in private life, Cicero had said, those who govern a republic ought

> to study the interest of their constituents, not that of those to whom the trust is committed. Those who consult the good of a party of the citizens, and neglect another part, introduce into society two pernicious things, sedition and discord; from this cause it always happens, that some are considered as the friend of the people, and others as wholly devoted to the rich and powerful. . . . From this source, arose mighty dissensions among the Athenians; and in our republic, not only seditions but destructive civil wars; evils, which a virtuous and courageous citizen, worthy to preside in the republic, would avoid and detest. Such a man will devote himself entirely to the republic . . . and he will protect all parts of the body politic, and consult the interests of all the citizens. Cicero de off. Lib. 1. cap. 25. Art. 85, 86. (3:147)

The Federalists' claim to be the party of Washington has sometimes been viewed as a mere rhetorical strategy, an attempt to win for themselves after his death a share in Washington's enormous prestige when alive. In fact it was a wholly genuine claim, against what they saw as the blandishments of Jeffersonian democratic republicanism, to be the party of *virtus* in Cicero's sense. The symbolic importance of Washington is that he was, for Federalists, the living embodiment of this principle.[4] "Washington's last address to the people," Fisher Ames would write, "is the solemn creed of federalists, which they approve in their hearts . . . and which they devoutly pray may be admitted by every honest citizen to his heart and affections" (*Works* 301). "He governed by no party," say the authors of a memorial to Washington published in *The Port Folio*. "He labored to raise up a spirit fit to cope with the passions which . . . have so often . . . extinguished the principles of a free government. He wished . . . to unite us in one common end—that we might be faithful to ourselves and to the state" (10:2:465).

The Port Folio's portrayal of Washington as the living spirit of the *virtus* of the ancient republics demonstrates the degree to which Federalism would remain loyal to the spirit of classical republican thought even in an age when new theories of progress seemed to have called into doubt all notions of human history as a cyclical process, the inevitable consequence of known causes working to known ends. The above account of civic virtue given by Cicero in *de Officiis*, for instance, occurs in *The Port Folio* as part of an extraordinary "History of the French Revolution by Ancient Writers" composed for the pages of *The Port Folio* by John Adams, then living in retirement on his farm in Quincy, Massachusetts. It is a running account of events in France, from the storming of the Bastille to the rise of Napoleon, as described by "a society of Latin writers" (Cicero, Sallust, Livy, Velleius Paterculus, Tacitus, Suetonius, Cornelius Nepos, Quintus Curtius)—really, of course, passages taken from these authors and arranged so as to seem to tell the story of the French Revolution.

To read the "History" as Adams compiled it is, even today, to have an eerie sense that history must after all be a process of cycles and repetitions, variations on known themes working themselves out according to certain permanent laws of human nature. To readers of the original *Port Folio*, for whom the French Revolution was still vivid in memory, the effect must have been uncannier still. Thus, for instance, Adams allows Tacitus to tell the story of Robespierre and the Terror. It is not the casual fact of murder and brutality—one does not need classical republican theory to tell one that these have always existed—but a certain poignancy of personal detail that convinces one that Tacitus must, so to speak, have been there in Paris: "To approach a relation or a friend, to weep over their misfortune, to give them a last look, was a crime. Guards, posted as spies, to watch for the smallest appearance of grief, attended the dead bodies, and dragged them to the river, where they were left to be carried down the stream. . . . No man dared to bury them, or come near them" (3:115).

The truth of Tacitus' *Annals*, in short, has to do not with events in ancient Rome or modern France but with a human nature that is only locally or trivially different in different epochs or cultures. Such works as Plutarch's *Lives*, says a writer in *The Port Folio*, demonstrate the validity of "Mr. Hume's observation, that the course of human events and the workings of the human mind are in all ages nearly the same" (5:20). This is the central moral axiom both of literary Augustanism and classical republican theory, one that might have been heard in the eighteenth century on almost the same terms from thinkers and writers as otherwise various as Hume and Johnson, Bolingbroke and Gibbon, Dryden and Goldsmith. To emphasize similarity at the level of events was to retain a sense of cyclical history as it had remained strong in England and America past midcentury. It was in the name of cyclical history, and the wisdom to be gained from it, that one pored over Plutarch and Rollin, took warning from Brown's *Estimate* or Burgh's *Remembrancer*. To emphasize the source of that similarity in a permanent or universal human nature—what this *Port Folio* writer calls "the workings of the human mind"—is, however, to penetrate to the level of moral reality underlying the cyclical theory itself.

At this deeper level, the point of Adams's compilations from Tacitus and the others will be not simply that human nature is everywhere the same, but that its sameness consists in just the proneness to weakness and error that one sees at work in human history as recounted by Thucydides or Tacitus, human motivation as described by Plato or St. Augustine. To imagine the shade of Tacitus present and taking notes in the Paris of Robespierre and the sansculottes—"Some, intoxicated with wine, marched without knowing why or where. The worst of men, abandoned to villainy, seized the opportunity to plunder" (3:90)—is merely to recognize that humanity contains within itself certain dark impulses over which civilization, whenever it has achieved peace and order and justice, constitutes a temporary and hard-won victory. This is not meant to imply, as so many modern readers have been disposed to hear the Federalists as arguing, that all men and women, or most of them, are irrational or violent. It is meant to insist, however, that when the lights go out and the laws have failed, there are in every human society those who will seize the opportunity to plunder.

For the *Port Folio* writers, the lesson of history is that the ideology of progress preached by the jacobins in Paris and the Jeffersonians in America—"the glorious work of that perfectibility of the species, foretold by Condorcet," as Fisher Ames contemptuously puts it[5]—is simply the newest version of the old lie preached by demagogues to the multitudes in Greece and Rome, the idea that nothing is wanted to abolish the unhappiness of the human condition except the unrestrained reign of the demos. The Federalist way of urging the lesson is always to insist that human moral nature was not one thing in the Greece of Thucydides or the Rome of Tacitus and another in Jefferson's America.[6] "Because the people of these states are . . . virtuous," says Warren Dutton in a Fourth of July speech given in Boston and published in *The Port Folio*, "they have been taught that they have no vices. But . . . it ought to be said with equal sincerity, that they are subject to like passions with other men. They consist of the rich and the poor, the simple and the wise, the idle and the industrious. . . . They have vanity, which may be flattered, and passions which can be excited" (5:219).

The Federalist sense of the past as a permanent source of civic wisdom gives us the meaning of the impassioned debate about classical learning carried on in the pages of *The Port Folio* from the first issue virtually to the last days of Dennie's editorship. At issue is classical learning precisely as exemplified in Adams's "History of the French Revolution by Ancient Authors." "By looking into history and seeing what has been," says Fisher Ames in words that might be taken as an epigraph for Adams's compilation, "we know what will be. It is thus that dumb experience speaks audibly; it is thus that witnesses come from the dead and testify" (*Works* 223). Adams's "History" teaches this lesson powerfully and explicitly. But it implicitly teaches another lesson as well, no less powerful by the lights of *The Port Folio's* Federalism—namely, that the republic has such wisdom available to it only when there are readers able to range freely through the Latin pages of Cicero and Suetonius and Cornelius Nepos.

The debate over classical learning in Jeffersonian America has been taken to be mainly a disagreement over educational policy (see Kerber 95–134), which are indeed the terms in which it was carried on. It has also been superbly analyzed by Robert Ferguson as underlying a crucial shift in the relation of law to literature in the early republic.[7] To grasp the urgency the subject possessed for Dennie and the *Port Folio* writers, however, one must see that it was for them also something more, a debate about the sources of civic virtue in modern society. For the Federalist ideal of classical learning involves not merely the notion of practical wisdom to be gained from reading ancient texts, Xenophon and Livy as guides to events in contemporary New York or Philadelphia, but also the idea of an actual transfer of virtue from the ancient republics to the modern world. This is something that comes about, on the Federalist view, only when a society includes educated readers as much at home in ancient Athens or Rome as in present-day New York or Philadelphia. This means not simply reading Xenophon and Livy, but having the ability to do so in Greek and Latin.

This is the part of the debate over classical learning that is hardest to grasp today, when a student reading Cicero would be likely to do so, if at all, in English translation. For the Federalist writers, however, the deepest value of classical learning was that it involves a sort of time travel in which the reader vanishes for a prolonged and privileged moment from his own time and place and reappears in the midst of ancient society, listening to Pericles addressing the Athenians or Cicero undertaking to warn the Romans about the evil machinations of Catiline. The utterance of the orator becomes in this context the embodiment of *virtus*, which had been the point of ancient theorists like Quintilian and Cicero himself in insisting that moral qualities are as important to the orator as mere technical skills. In times of great peril to the republic, as a writer puts it who has been analyzing in *The Port Folio* Cicero's great speeches against Catiline, "the soul of one man, becomes that of an whole assembly, and of all the people" (4:293). This is the essence of oratory as it had been understood by Demosthenes or Cicero, and as it will always be understood in *The Port Folio*.

In American public life, therefore, only classical learning can produce the orator or statesman able to transmit *virtus* to societies otherwise cut off from the ancient world as a source of civic wisdom. Thus Oliver Oldschool will greet an address given by John Quincy Adams, for instance, as itself a kind of moral exemplum, as important for its classical resonances as for its argument or message: "Let us hear no more of that plan of study, which should exclude the ancients. Mr. Adams writes with spirit, sense, and melody, because he has translated SALLUST, and meditated TACITUS" (2:238). In more perilous circumstances, the same ideal of classical learning is taken to produce the tremendous eloquence of Burke as he rises in the House of Commons to warn Englishmen against the French Revolution—the same eloquence which one may yet hear in Burke's *Reflections* or *Letter to a Noble Lord*, and which, as we shall see, gives him heroic stature in *The Port Folio*—or, in America, Fisher Ames as he struggles to his feet in the House of Representatives to deliver his legendary speech on Jay's Treaty.

There is an even more important consideration. For the Federalist writers, the great value of classical education is not simply that one learns in youth the Greek and Latin needed to read one's Thucydides or Livy, but that dwelling imaginatively in the ancient world during the crucial period of one's moral formation actually produces a different human being than would otherwise have existed. The theme is stressed repeatedly in the letters, serialized in *The Port Folio* in 1804, from William Pitt the Elder to his nephew at Oxford. For the Pitt who speaks here, Oliver Oldschool reminds his readers, is the living proof of his own theory of education, the great man who had led England out of the depths of post-Walpolian corruption to greatness in the Seven Years War, and whose impassioned eloquence in the House of Commons had made him seem the very soul of the English people. "You are already possessed of the true idea to guide you through this dangerous and perplexing part of your life's journey, the years of education," writes Pitt to his nephew, urging him to follow the "true clue" he already possesses: "the use of learning is, to render a man more wise and virtuous; not merely to make him more learned. Macte tua virtute" (4:314).

The deeper point of Pitt's exhortation emerges when a reader sees that its concept of "use" is very nearly oxymoronic, and is meant to be: the use of classical learning and the wisdom and virtue it encourages, in short, is precisely that they have no use, that in a world dominated by narrow self-interest and an unthinking obsession with means they represent, in a way upon which the philosophers of ancient Greece had always insisted, ends in themselves. *The Port Folio* will always dwell in the strongest terms on the special urgency of this message for Jeffersonian America. The maxims delivered by Pitt to his nephew, says Oliver Oldschool, should be taken to heart by "every studious youth in America": "they will not, it is true, teach the Way to Wealth by the rules of an exciseman's arithmetic. . . . But all readers, who . . . can taste and relish the ancient page, all to whom honor is a habit, and who estimate wisdom and nobleness of mind of higher worth, than wild land or stock in the Bank of the United States, will peruse and follow the advice of a CHATHAM" (4:313).

This is the context in which *The Port Folio* will always insist on an essential relation, very hard to grasp in modern terms but nonetheless essential to Federalist thought, between the simple ability to read Greek and Latin and the perpetuation of civic virtue in the nation. For in a society imaginatively dominated by money, whose guidebook is, as Oldschool says, Franklin's *The Way to Wealth,* and whose ideology is Jeffersonian individualism, the whole point of learning the ancient languages is that they demonstrate a living commitment to mind or intellect for no sake but their own. "Notoriously," says one *Port Folio* writer, author of a series of essays on "The Progress of Literature," "the characteristic spirit of our people is commercial, and wherever it predominates, pursuits, not auxiliary to its purposes, are in low estimation" (7:2:356). In *The Port Folio* during the years of Dennie's editorship this is a theme with endless variations, behind which may be felt a genuine and anguished conviction that in America an unrestrained economic individualism has become the mortal enemy of genuine learning.

For the Federalist writers, the symbolic value of Greek and Latin is that they cannot be learned without considerable effort, so that the study that simply permits one to read Livy or Tacitus may be taken as an allegory of learning for its own sake. This is why *The Port Folio* will so often portray classical learning in terms almost of religious vocation; "the secrecy in which they are withdrawn from vulgar notice," one writer will say about books in the ancient languages, "has something sacred in it" (8:2:398). Classically educated souls become in Federalist eyes the flamines or pontifices of a nation otherwise living by the maxims of Poor Richard, its custodians of the spirit of disinterested pursuit. In the new American republic, says a member of Dennie's old Walpole circle now writing in *The Port Folio*, "the whole soul is wrapped up in commercial speculation": "From these sources has sprung the party spirit, which disgraces our country. The mind cased up by these narrow prejudices, and bounded by the log-book, ledger, invoice, and policy of insurance, cannot judge aright on political questions" (1:291).

Throughout the years of Jefferson's presidency, *The Port Folio* feels itself to be locked into an invisible controversy with the proponents of democratic education. It is a bitter controversy, as the Federalist writers by the end come to understand Jeffersonian democracy as making war both on the notion of learning as a disinterested pursuit and on the idea of a classically educated minority, taught by its reading of ancient authors to mistrust the demos as an alien body within a truly democratic society. Nothing better catches *The Port Folio*'s sense of the real issues at stake, perhaps, than the gloomy irony of the North Carolina correspondent who reports that the "enlightened legislature" of his state has just stripped funds from the university because it has "discovered that education was inconsistent with republicanism; that it created an aristocracy of the learned, who would trample upon the rights and liberties of the ignorant, and that an equality of intellect was necessary to preserve the equality of rights" (6:2:360).

In the irony of this North Carolina correspondent may be heard the dying echoes of a lost ideological battle. For *The Port Folio* would never succeed in making the point that the "aristocracy" against which the Jeffersonians declaimed was imaginary or nonexistent in American, and that to rail against aristocracy could only be to indulge in demagoguery. Yet the Federalist writers were sincere believers in what Gordon Wood has called the radicalism of the American Revolution. The point of liberty under what one *Port Folio* writer calls "a republican form of government, in which no titles or privileges subsist" (3:154), the Federalist writers thought, must have entirely to do with the right to rise in society through one's own industry and the moral qualities that command the respect of one's neighbors. In America, says the *Port Folio* writer just quoted, "the people have all power, the humblest citizen may become the most exalted, and rulers be reduced to private station. Taxes are levied on all ranks alike, no order of men is more favored than another" (3:154). "True liberty," another will say, "consists in making every higher degree accessible to those who are in a lower, if virtue and talents are there found to deserve advancement" (6:2:267).

The Port Folio's emphasis on classical learning as a perennial source of civic virtue assumes the notion of a society in which real republican liberty depends, in a way utterly strange to modern ears, on maintaining distinctions of rank or status. For in a polity where some are made more prosperous than others by their energy and industry, the great danger is that social superiority will materialize as mere wealth, richer clothing and larger dwellings and crystal glassware and silver plate. This is the danger that in classical republican theory had always carried the name of Luxury, and that may be seen to threaten even virtuous republics when their *virtus* has carried them to a certain level of prosperity. For the Federalists, in fact, one great shame of Jeffersonian America is precisely that it recognizes no other measure of superiority than wealth; "the only avenue to consideration and importance in our society," says Fisher Ames, "is the accumulation of property; our inclinations cling to gold." But this is not all Jefferson and democracy. The very fluidity of American social arrangements, Ames observes regretfully, "favors the progress of luxury" (*Works* 35).

The remark occurs in Ames's much-anthologized essay on American literature, which has been so often read in isolation from his other writings that the classical republican meanings of his terms have been lost. Yet the emergence of literary Federalism cannot be understood without recovering those meanings. "Luxury" is one such term, of course, but another, as crucial precisely because of the solution it suggests to the problem of luxury within the classical republican paradigm, is "leisure" or "learned leisure," which Ames would have expected his readers instantly to recognize as the otium or *otium cum dignitate* of ancient poetry and philosophy. The advancement both of literature and knowledge in the United States, says Ames, "would require the learned leisure, which a numerous class enjoy in Europe, but which cannot be enjoyed in America." The reason why it cannot be enjoyed we have already heard: poetry and art and philosophy flourish only in societies where wealth serves the ends of otium rather than "mere appetite or ostentation," and the latter rule in Jeffersonian America.

The ideal of otium or "literary leisure," as Ames also calls it in this essay, lies at the heart of Federalist values precisely as it operates to sustain civic virtue even while a republic is increasing in wealth and populousness. For otium, still carrying associations with Aristotle's theory of leisure as the basis of genuine civilization, is the negation of wealth pursued for the purpose of appetite or ostentation. To use excess income to fill one's library with Homer and Virgil and Horace, to work in order to buy oneself the time and freedom to read poetry and history and philosophy, to give to study and contemplation the hours the busy world spends on empty frivolity, is in Federalist eyes not simply to forswear luxury but to provide a moral antidote to it. "Nothing, in my opinion," says Oliver Oldschool, "would more promote the substantial glory of the country, than a wide diffusion of classical literature" (2:261), and what he has in mind is not simply the Aeneid or Horace's *Sermones* but the idea of otium.

The otium ideal explains as well *The Port Folio*'s idealization of Alexander Hamilton, who becomes the hero of its Federalism not only because of his role in the Revolutionary War and the first federal administration under Washington, but also because his vision of a republic in which public credit becomes a new kind of property in the nation. For Oliver Oldschool and his contributors, the Hamiltonian notion of public credit will be the equivalent under American conditions of landed status in the England of classical republican theory, important primarily as it provides the conditions of civic virtue. These are the conditions Hamilton would have seemed to them to have obviously in mind when he speaks, in an address published in *The Port Folio*, of "the sober maxims on which our federal edifice was reared." The effect of those maxims, he declares with a measure of justified pride, have been "an extension of our commerce and manufactures, the rapid growth of our cities and towns, the consequent prosperity of agriculture. . . . All this was effected, by giving life and activity to a capital in the public obligations, which was before dead" (1:169).

This relation between Hamilton's vision of the American republic and the otium ideal is visible partly because *The Port Folio* views Hamilton himself as the highest product of classical education (Pitt's "Macte tua virtute"), but also because his conception of public credit as property in the nation seems so obviously to promise the conditions under which otium might thrive, thus ensuring a perpetual supply of future Hamiltons to guide the destiny of the republic. This is the vision that dies with Hamilton. Nowhere is *The Port Folio*'s sense of permanent loss more poignantly caught, perhaps, than in a commencement oration spoken after Hamilton's death by a student at the University of Pennsylvania, a young American looking back from the shrunken Jeffersonian world of democratic demagoguery and land-jobbing to the early days of the Washington administration:

At the successful conclusion of the American Revolution . . . we were found to be—an exhausted, distracted, and divided people. . . . Jealousies, rancorous jealousies, kept individuals asunder, and fearful rivalships separated the states, each part was afraid of the whole, and no common exertion could be excited for the common good. The eye of Hamilton surveyed this fermenting chaos of ruinous confusion, and he spoke it into energy and order. . . . He forced the American people to know that their safety was in union; and dispelled the misty doubts, the mean suspicions, which had brought them to the brink of ruin. . . . How instantly we rose, under his creating hand to a giant's size, the world has witnessed with astonishment. (7:2:77)

Beyond Hamilton's greatness as a soldier and statesman, there is the majesty of his role as spokesman for Federalist principles after the death of Washington, the sort of public eloquence that looks back to the oratory of Demosthenes or Cicero in the ancient world, and in the modern age puts him in the company of Pitt during the Seven Years War or Burke in the early years of the French Revolution. This again is an eloquence always associated by *The Port Folio* with classical learning, as when Oliver Oldschool remarks that he reads and rereads "Burke's eloquent phillipic against the French revolution . . . not merely for its rhetoric, which rivals that of Rome, but for its political truth, which is the echo of ages" (3:43). The Hamilton whom we heard addressing the electors of New York—"To what end, fellow-citizens, has your attention been carried across the Atlantic, to the revolution of France . . . ? To what end are you told, that this is . . . a war between equal and unequal rights, between republicanism and monarchy, between liberty and tyranny?" (1:163)—is thus, like Burke in England, the very voice of *virtus* in a world decomposing into democracy and mob rule.

Even as *The Port Folio* is attempting to reassure itself by seeing Hamilton as an orator on the ancient model, however, the French Revolution has begun to render unreal the idea of the polis from which the model derives in classical republican thought. For Hamilton warning Americans about the French Revolution is not a Demosthenes or a Cicero addressing a small and homogeneous community of political equals but, precisely because his remarks insist on Jeffersonianism as a variant of French radical doctrines, an actor in a single cosmic drama being played out on both sides of the Atlantic. This explains why the tone of *The Port Folio* during this period, even when its focus is on American politics as such, will so often border on the apocalyptic. "There is yet a body of principles among us," says one of its writers in 1804, that might save the nation from the "yawn of destruction"; the moment has arrived for the politically uninvolved to choose sides. These "must, if they perish, perish in one grave, the grave which Anarchy is digging for our Commonwealth and has dug for so many Commonwealths before us" (4:236).

The power of the French Revolution to dissolve the claims of nation and local community—the point of Tocqueville's famous remark that "the French Revolution had no country"—had been felt in America almost from the moment of the storming of the Bastille, so that the Oldschool perspective is virtually from the beginning one in which local allegiances demand evaluation in global terms. In succeeding years one has increasingly a sense of *The Port Folio*'s horizons expanding to take in a transatlantic anti-jacobin community: Gifford and the *Anti-Jacobin* writers in England, the early *Edinburgh Review* group in Scotland, the *Salmagundi* authors in New York, orators and statesmen like Burke and William Windham in Britain and Gouverneur Morris and Hamilton and Fisher Ames in the United States, the anti-jacobin Irish poet Tom Moore, already a favorite of *The Port Folio* for his Anacreontic odes, as he visits Dennie and his circle in Philadelphia.

The symbolic relation between classical learning and civic virtue in Federalist thought is epitomized in *The Port Folio*'s portrayal of Edmund Burke, whose emergence as a dominant voice in the magazine has to do with his early clairvoyant sense of the French Revolution as a cosmic drama, and with his courage in having denounced the revolutionaries at a time when the rest of Europe was still singing their praises. Burke threw off every tainted connection, says one *Port Folio* writer, thinking of his earlier association with men like Charles James Fox, "by boldly unfurling a radiant flag of warfare against the demoniac enemy of social being. . . . Mr. Burke was the first to foresee, and predict, the devouring and desolating effects of that tremendous explosion on morals, religion, and law. At a moment of general infatuation, he had the hardy resolution . . . with a warning voice, to expose to mankind the rocks, and quick-sands, and siren perils of that destructive sea" (1:123). The writer's language is itself Burkean. Nothing better suggests the nature of Burke's symbolic importance to *The Port Folio* than these images of storm and sea, the French Revolution as something more nearly resembling a natural cataclysm than a political event.

For the literary Federalists, Burke's greatness lay in his having derived from classical republican tradition an idea of organic community able to serve as a common point of reference for everyone in the imaginary intellectual country Tocqueville said was brought into being by the French Revolution. For what classical republican theory had perceived in Periclean Athens or the early Roman republic, privileged periods of collective harmony and purpose in which citizens had chosen to live for the community rather than only for themselves, could now in Burkean terms be seen as a potentiality within any human society. This was the basis of Burke's great countervision of the social contract in *Reflections in the Revolution in France,* insisting against Locke and Rousseau that society can only be understood as a vast mutual system of rights and responsibilities. Dennie reprints the famous passage in *The Port Folio* in 1807:

> Society is indeed a contract. Subordinate contracts for objects of mere occasional interest may be dissolved at pleasure—but the state ought not to be considered as nothing better than a partnership agreement in a trade of pepper and coffee, calico or tobacco, or some other such low concern, to be taken up for a little temporary interest. . . . It is a partnership in all science; a partnership in all art; a partnership in every virtue, and in all perfection. As the ends of such a partnership cannot be obtained in many generations, it becomes a partnership not only between those who are living, but between those who are living, those who are dead, and those who are to be born. Each contract of each particular state is but a clause in the great primeval contract of eternal society, linking the lower with the higher natures, connecting the visible and invisible world, according to a fixed compact sanctioned by the inviolable oath which holds all physical and all moral natures, each in their appointed place. (7:1:75–76)

To European readers of Burke's *Reflections,* these words had signaled a break or rupture within classical republican tradition, an announcement that the French Revolution had brought into being a new international order in which nations would no longer be able to sustain themselves with a simple hope of returning to an earlier, more virtuous stage of their own development. To *The Port Folio* and its American readers, the same lesson would dawn more gradually as a growing awareness that America in the age of the printing press and global commerce belongs to a single vast transatlantic community. Thus there appears in *The Port Folio* in 1805, for instance, an essay on the Gutenberg revolution that today might stand as an epigraph to Habermas's theory of the public sphere as we shall encounter it in chapter 4. The prestige of the orator in the ancient polis, the essayist is saying, had been due entirely to the absence of the printed word: "when books were so scarce, as they must have been before the invention of printing," citizens could not "read the speeches of great men in their closets, but were obliged to crowd the forum, or public place of assembly. There they listened to the orator as to an oracle" (5:294).

Today, however, printed texts go everywhere. This is why Burke at a certain point begins to be heard in the pages of *The Port Folio* as a Demosthenes or Cicero of the modern public sphere, the commanding voice of an age when great men are able to speak to readers in their closets—that is, studies or private libraries—and to do so, moreover, across the divisions of time and place and nationality. The imaginary community summoned into existence by Burke's eloquence is always envisioned by Oliver Oldschool and the *Port Folio* writers as suspended above national borders, composed of all those readers who share Burke's perception, and their own, of the French Revolution as an episode in what must now be grasped as a symbolic struggle over the fate of genuine civilization. This is the context in which *The Port Folio* begins to understand itself as the voice of an invisible community sustained primarily by moral allegiances, in which a Federalist in America and an anti-jacobin in England and a French émigré who has fled the Terror have far more in common with one another than with those in their respective countries who persist in sympathizing with the French Revolution.

Along with Burke, *The Port Folio* increasingly turns to the thought and writings of the members of Burke's literary and intellectual circle, especially Samuel Johnson and Oliver Goldsmith. For as time passes, Oliver Oldschool and his contributors begin also to realize that the symbolic warfare in which they are engaged today had, in effect, been going on throughout the entire eighteenth century, with the forces of Enlightenment skepticism—Voltaire, Diderot, Helvetius, Holbach, and a thousand minor philosophes—ranged against such men as Burke and Johnson and Goldsmith. Thus Johnson, for instance, long in eclipse even among Federalists because of his opposition to the American cause at the time of the Revolution, will reemerge in the pages of *The Port Folio* as the mighty spokesman for the Augustinian view of a human nature that is everywhere, in all ages and climes and occupations and social classes, essentially the same. "He seemed to stand alone," says one *Port Folio* writer, "on the theater of our world, as a giant of forbidding and turbulent aspect. . . . Fearless, ardent, persevering, anxious, unremitting, he encountered error in all its shapes . . . and vice trembled at his approach in all her lurking places. Such was Johnson" (5:289).

The first great move towards a Federalism whose values will be literary rather than political occurs as *The Port Folio* takes as its own imaginative center England in the age of Johnson, in which it comes to see a last prolonged interlude of literature and wit and conversation before the storm of the French Revolution burst to alter forever the conditions of European intellectual life. The great value of the Johnson circle for the *Port Folio* writers is precisely the way its members had succeeded in creating through language counterworlds to Enlightenment skepticism: Boswell's *Life of Johnson* with its image of Johnson as the mighty symbolic antagonist of Voltaire and Hume and Rousseau, Johnson himself as author of *Rasselas* or *The Rambler*, works of deep humanity nonetheless insisting on a perpetual human proneness to error and self-deception, Goldsmith as the master of a new age of polite literature in which style continuously draws its magic, as in such works as *The Deserted Village* or *The Vicar of Wakefield*, from the memory of an older world of simple manners and immemorial custom.

After Burke's death *The Port Folio* embraces as his successor William Windham of Norfolk, "a brilliant member of that literary club, in which Dr. Johnson, Edmund Burke, &c so long mingled," as Oliver Oldschool approvingly notes in 1802. Even as he is heard in *The Port Folio* as a statesman in the Burkean mold, however, Windham shows that he has arrived at certain conclusions about the French Revolution that Burke himself did not live long enough to grasp. For to have lived to see victorious Napoleonic armies spreading across Europe is to understand that the explanation of events since the storming of the Bastille does not lie, after all, in radical French doctrines of abstract rights, that these, like Napoleon himself, have been produced by certain deeper forces at work in the modern world. Windham's own sense that these have to do with what Marx would later call underlying material conditions is most often expressed as a warning to his countrymen about commerce and the pursuit of wealth: "Before capital and commerce were known, our ancestors . . . held the first rank among the nations of Europe," he says in a speech reprinted in *The Port Folio*. But today, "basely hugging our money bags, we think we may dismiss the military virtues of our forefathers" (2:143).

This is the very voice of Oliver Oldschool's Federalism, which in the American context becomes a warning that "the rage for amassing money," as he once calls it, "our truly American covetousness" (1:231), is rapidly laying waste to every noble or disinterested pursuit in the new nation, that literature and art and philosophy and civic virtue have together been doomed in a Jeffersonian democracy ruled, as another *Port Folio* writer says, by a "rage for vulgar popularity, and for amassing gold rather than ideas" (7:1:385). Thus it is, for instance, that the terms of Windham's remarks to the British House of Commons ("hugging our money bags") will be directly echoed in a letter reprinted in *The Port Folio* from a European immigrant who, having come to the United States in hopes of finding a society animated by republican virtue, had discovered instead a nation "engrossed by commercial speculations": "growing heartily weary of the land of liberty, and vulgar aristocracy, seated on her bags of dollars," the writer says, he ended by resolving to return to Europe (1:150).

The reason that Alexander Hamilton emerges as the symbol of *The Port Folio*'s Federalism has ultimately to do with Hamilton's sense, most nearly resembling that of Burke or Windham in England, that the French Revolution has inaugurated a genuinely new epoch in human history and that the history of America will, no matter what the wishes of her people or her political leaders, be played out on a world stage on which impersonal forces, most notably including those of what we have heard Windham call capital and commerce, will determine the ultimate conditions of national greatness. During the early years of Dennie's editorship, of course, there would be a fatal division within Federalism between the opposing visions of Hamilton and John Adams. Yet the disappearance of Adams from the pages of *The Port Folio* does not represent any taking of political sides by Dennie or the magazine. It is simply the fading away of an older classical republicanism, Country party notions of cyclical history and luxury and corruption, in favor of that newer Burkean vision whose point is always to try to preserve classical republican values in a world now undergoing transformation by the blind forces of a global system of credit and commerce.

The sudden news of Hamilton's death, when it comes to *The Port Folio*, involves a sense of tragic loss having as much to do with the republic as with the man. Even today, a reader turning over the pages of the magazine encounters with almost personal shock the black-bordered number for 21 July 1804, mourning both the death of Hamilton and the fate of his "afflicted country, bereaved of her brightest, greatest, and most steadfast hope" (4:229). The account of the silent crowds lining the streets at his funeral is, by the same token, an image of a citizenry carried back to the early days of the republic: "It renewed their grief for the death of Washington, to see his friend and counselor cut off in the highest vigor of his faculties, and the United States deprived of their great earthly stay. Immediately after his decease the bells announced that the was no more. On the morning of the day of his funeral, all the bells were muffled, and tolled from six to seven o'clock. . . . The bells again tolled from seven to eight in the evening" (4:230).

The dominant note in Federalist mourning is the notion of Hamilton as classical republican hero, the embodiment of military *virtus* in time

47

of war, the statesman and orator who through the power of his moral presence had done so much to preserve the virtue of the republic in time of peace. This is a note caught by Fisher Ames in a memorial written shortly after Hamilton's death; he was, says Ames, a patriot such as "the best Romans in their best days would have admitted to citizenship and to the consulate." "The most substantial glory of a country," Ames warns elsewhere in the same eulogy, "is in its virtuous great men. . . . That nation is fated to ignominy and servitude, for which such men have lived in vain" (*Works* 518). The same point is made simply and grandly by Oliver Oldschool in *The Port Folio* by letting stand as a comment on Hamilton's death the moving words of Tacitus on Agricola: "Quidquid ex illo amavimus, quidquid mirati sumus manet, mansurumque est in animus hominum, in aeternitate fama rerum. Nam multos veterum velut inglorios et ignobiles oblivio obruet. Ille posteritati narratus et traditus, superstes erit" (4:232).

The notion of Hamilton as Agricola, the virtuous Roman living on into a shrunken age of venality and low concerns, gives us the view of Jeffersonian America that will then be carried forward into the later years of *The Port Folio*, along with its related sense that the triumph of French revolutionary doctrine in the United States is not, after all, to be carried out in stormings of the Bastille or massacres of the nobility but rather as the long, slow erosion of civilized values in the name of the sovereign people and the common man. This is the context in which, after Hamilton's death, the role of Federalist Agricola will be assumed in the pages of *The Port Folio* by Fisher Ames. During the early years of *The Port Folio*, Ames had been most often heard as a voice imported from the *Palladium*, whose presiding spirit he is universally known to be. After the death of Hamilton, he is then heard as a voice speaking from otium retirement or retreat, living among his books and looking out upon a declining world, having become a sort of American Tacitus who, as a *Port Folio* sketch of the Roman author once says, had chosen to dwell in "the delightful retreat which literature always provides to the virtuous in their disappointments" (7:1:5).

When Ames's voice in turn falls into silence, there is thus felt within *The Port Folio* an almost involuntary shiver, as though the death of Federalism and its classical republican vision of America, though before perhaps felt to be imminent, has now taken place. Oldschool's eulogy of Ames is in great part almost perfunctory, as though spoken by someone in shock: "Mr. Ames was a firm believer in the political creed of Gen. Hamilton, and this, in our opinion, is the true faith. . . . On all the great questions of foreign or domestic polity, which have been . . . so darkly understood since the French Revolution, his opinions were consistent and correct." Only then does there creep in the note of that despair that will ultimately impel the Federalist retreat: "The extinction of such a light leaves us in a sort of melancholy gloom, and as when the lamp of Hamilton's life expired, even the stout hearted may shrink for a moment, while meditating upon the probable storm, or the coming night" (8:2:62).

This gloomy resignation marks the beginning of the Federalist retreat from history, a turning away from the noisy world of Jeffersonian America to an alternative sphere of literary imagination. It is now that the idea of classical learning, the wisdom of Aristotle or Cicero or Tacitus as a perpetual moral resource in the modern age, undergoes in *The Port Folio* a final transmutation. For now the writings that had once inspired Burke or Hamilton to public eloquence, or that had been able to sustain Fisher Ames in otium retirement, begin to appear in another light altogether, as a last permanent sanctuary from Jeffersonian democracy. For readers who have awakened to find themselves imprisoned in Jeffersonian America, may still, as Oliver Oldschool points out, escape into their books. In the pages of Virgil or Cicero or Shakespeare they may still "listen to all the pleadings of Eloquence, profit by the counsels of Wisdom, and partake of the triumph of Wit. Generous spirits may here forget the deformities of their country, crippled by a faulty government and correspondent manners, and turn indignant eyes from loathsome objects to the contemplation of virtuous and wise men, and better ages" (7:2:323).

Chapter Three

The Philosophy of Merriment

THE idea of reading as escape into a timeless realm, what Thomson in *The Seasons* calls "high converse with the mighty dead," had always been a major theme in English literary Augustanism. As *The Port Folio* in the later years of Dennie's editorship moves imaginatively backwards into an Augustan past, the theme assumes greater and greater importance as the Federalist writers begin to realize that they have not, after all, merely been opposing Jefferson or radical French doctrines but something incalculably larger and more inexorable, the tide of historical change as such. "We are in a gulf stream," Fisher Ames had written to a friend as early as 1803, "which has hitherto swept us along with more force than our sails and oars. . . . I will fatten my pigs, and prune my trees; nor will I any longer be at the trouble to govern this country. I am no Atlas, and my shoulders ache" (*Works* 1476). Within a few years, Dennie and his contributors will have drawn an identical conclusion.

This is the context in which the crucial element in *The Port Folio*'s retreat into literature as a separate sphere of reality becomes the illness of Joseph Dennie—not the chronic weakness of health suffered by the real Dennie, but that ill health as projected in the personae of the Lay Preacher and Oliver Oldschool, drawing on a tradition of literary valetudinarianism in which physical suffering brings with it a certain inescapable moral perspective on one's way of being in the world. The rise of the aesthetic begins in *The Port Folio* as an element in what Dennie himself once called the philosophy of merriment. "It is related of Henry Fielding," says Oldschool, "that when he was martyred with the gout . . . he used to read Seneca, and Cicero de Consolatione"; but "when we are rendered more than usually grave, by the 'dull realities' of this miserable life, it seems absurd to read grave authors, to make us still graver. . . . Monsieur St. Evremond recommends authors, who can excite us to laughter; and imagines Don Quixote, a better assuager of care, than Plutarch" (2:410).

The notion of illness or disease will gradually expand in *The Port Folio* to become a metaphor for America under Jeffersonian democracy—later in the passage just quoted Oldschool lists "the degradation of my country" as one source of his own recurrent melancholy—but its initial importance is precisely that it is apolitical. For physical illness is something so immediately and absorbingly present to consciousness that, in the misery of the present moment, worries about Jefferson or the French Revolution or Duane and *The Aurora* seem unreal, the mere diversions of people taking normal good health for granted and having the luxury of looking about for things to occupy their minds. Especially in the early years of *The Port Folio*'s bitter opposition to Jefferson, the effect is to backlight even passionate political controversy with a somber awareness that politics belongs, after all, to the passing show of a world caught up in its own bustle and self-importance, that in the end the paths of statesman and orator and Federalist editor alike lead but to the grave.

The valetudinarianism of the Lay Preacher and Oliver Oldschool is at the most fundamental level *The Port Folio*'s equivalent of the medieval Dance of Death or the *memento mori* of the Renaissance, the flickering midnight candle and the skull upon the table and the knowledge, grasped in an instant of intensely personal insight, that these eyes that are even now looking upon the skull are themselves gazing out from bony sockets. The perspective thus implied is nowhere better caught, perhaps, than in a paragraph addressed by Dennie to readers of *The Port Folio* early in 1812. There are, he observes, describing his own usual situation, "very few conditions more to be regretted than that of an active mind, laboring under the weight of a distempered body."

The sufferer lies down, delighted with the thoughts of tomorrow, pleases his Ambition with the Fame he shall acquire, or his Benevolence with the Good he shall impart. But in the night the skies are overcast, the temper of the air is changed, he wakes in languor, impatience and distraction, and has no longer any wish but for ease, nor any attention but to misery. It may be said that Disease generally begins that equality, which Death completes; the distinctions, which set one man so much above another, are very little perceived in the gloom of a sick chamber, where it will be vain to expect entertainment from the gay, or instruction from the wise; where all human glory is obliterated, the wit is clouded, the reasoner perplexed, and the hero subdued; where the highest and brightest of mortal beings finds nothing left him but the consciousness of innocence. (12:1:90)

By the time this passage actually appeared in *The Port Folio* Dennie was dead. Having recovered, as he thought, from an especially severe illness of the preceding autumn, filled by the return of health and spirits with optimistic plans for the magazine, he had suddenly and unexpectedly died just before the publication of the January issue. He was forty-four years old. A sense of the disbelief still felt by the members of his literary circle can be gotten from the hastily composed mortuary notice that appears in February. "With a mind restored to ease," recalls the anonymous memorialist, "and a heart returning to all its affections, his friends gladly hailed the renewed and vigorous exertions of his genius. But it was only the hectic strength that wrestles over the tomb. On these bright and cherished expectations the grave has suddenly closed" (12:2:186). Yet in an important sense, that grave, serving in *The Port Folio* much the same purpose of *memento mori* as the graveyard scene in *Hamlet*, had been gaping open since the earliest days of the magazine, so that its closing over Dennie now comes only as an event long foretold.

The theme of *memento mori* governs not simply Dennie's self-portrayal as the Lay Preacher or Oliver Oldschool but his selection of materials, original and reprinted. Thus, for instance, *The Port Folio* in 1805 reprints from a British publication a "Life of Graeme," a Scots poet so obscure that his fame in his lifetime had scarcely reached beyond his own locality. Only when we realize that Graeme is going to die young, and that he knows he is going to die, do we suddenly grasp the point of the selection. "I need not tell you," writes Graeme to a friend, "I am day by day approaching to the perfection of leanness, a skeleton. I have not a pair of stockings that will clap to my legs, and my breeches are become the very picture of Captain Bobadil's. A kind of pale yellow has taken possession of the hollow of my cheeks" (5:316). The point, as the brave jauntiness of Graeme's self-caricature suggests, has to do with what might be called literary dying, the way in which a mind sustained by literature is prepared to look with a certain amused detachment even upon the prospect of death.

The literary lineage to which Graeme's posture belongs goes back to Pope in the earlier eighteenth century—that Pope who in the *Epistle to Arbuthnot* speaks with cheerful unconcern of "this long disease, my life"—and may already be glimpsed in the letters written by Dennie as a young Harvard graduate, epistolary exercises in which we see him trying on the poses out of which will develop the Lay Preacher and Oliver Oldschool. "My health is frail," he writes his parents from Charleston, New Hampshire, in 1791. "There is no counteracting nature. . . . My cough is troublesome and my imagination is too often conjuring up specters." But then, as though in direct anticipation of his later philosophy of merriment, the sturdy disclaimer: "From this shaded picture don't suppose that my life is unhappy, my situation ineligible, or society unpleasant. No, these feelings are the pains and penalties to which at least my flesh is heir" (*Letters* 74).

In *The Lay Preacher* and *The Port Folio* we shall always see Dennie dwelling in a world in which death is not a punctual event but a protracted process, Death the allegorical companion of one's every waking hour. In eighteenth-century English literature the same theme gives us the Pope of the Horatian poems and Sterne as he appears in *A Sentimental Journey* or Fielding in *A Voyage to Lisbon*. The theme is as old as Epictetus: the ethical wisdom of treating each new day as one's last on earth. This is how the *memento mori* theme in *The Port Folio* will translate ultimately into a sense that what Dennie calls "the puppet-show of this world" (3:178) is unreal, the delusion of souls who have never felt, like Pope or Sterne or Dennie himself, the daily pang of their own mortality. In *The Port Folio*, where the puppet show is the raw bustle of Jeffersonian democracy, the same perspective will lead to the magazine's eventual retreat from politics or history.

The great exemplar of the philosophy of merriment in *The Port Folio* is Sterne's Parson Yorick, whose very name is meant to keep us in mind of the graveyard scene in *Hamlet* and thereby of the possibility of merriment in a world otherwise given over to anxiety or gloom. Yorick, says Oliver Oldschool, "danced with Death a merrier dance than any of those painted by Holbein. . . . When Death knocked at his door in London, Yorick flew to the banks of the Garonne, and although the frightful specter was clattering at his heels, this fellow of infinite jest, of most excellent fancy, preserved his good humor and pleasantry the whole way, as completely as the gayest of the gay inhabitants of the country" (3:179). In *The Port Folio*, Yorick's merry dance with death is reborn as Oliver Oldschool's humor and pleasantry in the face of mortal illness, a determination to go on living and laughing and enjoying one's books and the company of one's friends until the clattering at the door should prove to be, as it does for Dennie in the twelfth year of *The Port Folio*, the frightful specter of Death at last caught up with his victim.

As it relates to *The Port Folio*'s break with politics, in short, the philosophy of merriment does not represent some mere turning away from history toward frivolity and mirth, but continuous engagement with death as nonbeing, that limit of life or mortal consciousness that in both philosophy and Judeo-Christian theology has always been taken to provide the ultimate measure of the value of earthly things.

"In walking through the wilderness of this world," says Dennie in one of his *Farrago* essays, "our sense is oftener wounded by the thorn than regaled by the rose." This is the context in which merriment in *The Port Folio* must always be taken in a wholly unparadoxical sense to be the most serious of moral or ethical postures, not as abdication or escape but as a kind of spiritual warfare with the miseries of human existence: "By laughing, we shall lighten the load. Surly Care is not proof against ridicule. His intrusions are invited by our frowns, but mirth is the surest method to vanquish our foe" (1:66).

This notion of mirth or merriment as spiritual warfare, already traceable in the earliest numbers of *The Lay Preacher*, will eventually come to dominate the literary ethos of *The Port Folio* as a whole, not just the portions written by Dennie but those by his contributors, and in time will come to redefine everything—religion, politics, literature—in relation to its own cardinal principle of cheerfulness in the face of woe. "Why," the Lay Preacher once asks, posing the central axiom of the philosophy of merriment in the words of Ecclesiastes, "shouldst thou die before thy time": "be of good cheer . . . nor impertinently inquire of Mirth what doeth she, but believe with my predecessor, Sterne, that comfortable assertion is worth a million of cold homilies, that every time we smile, and still more, every time we laugh, it adds something to the fragment of life" (6:1:65).

The movement through which Dennie's own illness will come to serve as a metaphor for America under Jeffersonian democracy, his philosophy of merriment as a warrant for *The Port Folio*'s retreat from history into a world of the literary imagination, begins in a certain revision of Augustinian Christianity that, while leaving intact the notion of Original Sin and a fallen human state, will repudiate as an egregious misreading of God's intent the Calvinistic severity of Puritan theology in both New England and Britain. The symbolic importance of Sterne in this context becomes not simply his cheerfulness in the face of death, but its entire consonance with the cheerful Christianity of a more orthodox Anglicanism. Thus, for instance, we hear Oliver Oldschool agreeing with Gray's remark that "Sterne in his sermons appears to be always on the verge of laughter," but with an important proviso: "there are graver divines than he, and of high repute in the church, who have indulged themselves in a strain of pulpit jocularity" (3:157).

The serious point of such jocularity emerges whenever *The Port Folio* has occasion to deal with the excesses of intolerance carried out in the name of Puritan godliness, or with the harm done to individual believers by the iron tenets of a rigid Calvinism. This is a theme that arises again and again in connection with Cowper, who, as the last great poet of elegiac Augustanism, is, along with Goldsmith and Thomas Moore, one of the main heroes of *The Port Folio*'s literary Federalism, but who is seen as having been driven to the very extremity of mental distress by Calvin's doctrine of predestination. Thus, for instance, Cowper as he appears in *The Port Folio* in a biographical sketch by a personal acquaintance, brought to the brink of suicide by a conviction that he was born to be damned: "Mr. Madan convinced him, that all mankind were on the same level with himself before God; the atonement and righteousness of Christ were set forth to him as the remedy which his ease required. . . . His mind derived present ease from these important truths" (1:125).

When Cowper's suicidal gloom returns, as it almost immediately does, we are to see in his predicament not some local derangement but the irrationality of extreme Calvinism itself, the dark impulse of that Puritanism that had plunged England into civil war and, during the blessedly short period of its reign in America, had warped the moral character of New England. Here is Cowper, the pitiable emblem of all who have been unable to see that God, while just, is also a God of mercy: "The following day, he again sunk under the horrors of perdition; . . . A vein of self-loathing ran through the whole of his insanity; and his faculties were so completely deranged, that the attempt, which he had lately deplored as an unpardonable transgression, now appeared to him an indispensable work of piety. He, therefore, repeated his assault upon his own life, under the dreadful delusion, that it was right to rid the earth of such a sinner" (1:125).

The Port Folio's answer to such gloomy imaginings, contained at first in isolated numbers of *The Lay Preacher* but eventually echoed in virtually every department of the magazine, will always be that the fallen world into which we are born due to Adam's sin is itself the punishment that was promised to our first parents, and that Christianity is nothing other than the ray of cheer or comfort sent to guide us through its wilderness of pain and misery. "I am persuaded," says the Lay Preacher in a wholly typical utterance, "that christianity was designed to be a cheerful system. Miserable was the perversion of its precepts by those, in early times, who believed that none could be its sincere votaries, but the moping and the austere. . . . Not to be too anxious, to hope habitually, to enjoy soberly, and to rejoice evermore are prominent precepts in the New Testament" (5:275). This is the theology of cheerfulness always meant to be glimpsed even in *The Lay Preacher*'s occasional moments of Shandean levity.

As *The Lay Preacher* continues as a series in *The Port Folio*, however, Sterne and Parson Yorick begin to fade in favor of a more explicitly religious model: St. Paul as he had been an apostle to the Gentiles in the earliest period of Christianity, and who in Dennie's reconception of that role becomes an apostle not simply of cheerful Christianity but of polite learning, of wit and literature and taste. It is one of the oddest and yet the most significant movements in early American writing, this process through which Dennie speaks in the accents of his own version of Pauline Christianity to an America unconverted to literature and learning, and then, as though belatedly noticing what he has done, sets about re-creating the St. Paul of the New Testament in the image of the Lay Preacher: "Polished by all the refinement of liberal studies, he seems to be entirely at home, in the circles of literature and genius. The poetry, the philosophy, and the theology of the times are perfectly familiar to him. . . . He was the Jewish Aristippus" (8:1:34).

At such moments Paul comes to appear in *The Port Folio* not only as the patron saint of cheerful Christianity, or of the values of civility and taste, but of an older organic society yet surviving in America in isolated pockets amidst the brawl and bustle of Jeffersonian democracy. The symbol of this society, taken as such precisely because the Puritans had always denounced Christmas as a vestige of popish superstition and episcopal tyranny, is the traditional Yuletide of the New England countryside. Already in Dennie's description may be felt the moral nostalgia of Irving's Christmas stories or the early Dickens: "When I cast my eye upon the vivid evergreen, that decks the Church at this festal season; when I see many happy and benevolent faces, lightening up before me; when I listen, with rapture, to the organist, and behold a caroling Christmas, with blended dignity and gaiety in his air, I am naturally led to reflect that Christianity is a cheerful religion" (7:2:410).

The essence of the Lay Preacher's notion of cheerful Christianity is that amidst pain and misery and sin and error there remains the saving thought, inculcated by Paul and Augustine and embodied in Christian teaching through successive ages, that mortal existence is but an exile from which God is summoning us to an eternal return. The point is especially important because those who do not see Christian truth this way include "those unhappy Puritans," as the Lay Preacher puts it, who had imagined Christianity to be a matter of "austere penance, whining tones, and a sad countenance" (7:2:410). This is the perversion of true Christianity which *The Port Folio* identifies specifically with the militant Puritanism of the English interregnum. Obey, says the Lay Preacher to his imaginary congregation, the cheerful "precepts of primitive Christians, who are of higher authority than John Pym, or Praise God Barebones, or Oliver Cromwell, although these stupid schismatics, ridiculously called themselves a Gospel preaching Ministry" (7:2:411).

The importance of Cromwell and the Puritan ascendancy in seventeenth-century England, apart from their obvious connections to New England Puritanism, is that they are taken in *The Port Folio* to be a prefiguration of Jacobinism in revolutionary France and Jeffersonian democracy in America, a zealotry that comes from mistaking the wilderness of the world for one's true home and then, guided by one's misery and discontent, reimagining it in the image of one's own shifting and selfish desire. This is, as we have seen, the sense in which the sin of Satan in Genesis or *Paradise Lost* may be glimpsed behind the turbulence and anarchy of the demos in ancient Athens or Rome, and its inevitable tendency is to dissolve the bonds of society such that a single overmastering spirit, a Pisistratus or a Caesar or a Cromwell or a Napoleon, at last emerges from the turbulence to restore order through naked force. This is the context in which Praise God Barebones and Citizen Robespierre may be taken as kindred spirits beneath the surface.

Though *The Port Folio*'s philosophy of merriment will resolve itself into an Anacreontic posture that some contemporary readers mistook for mere shallow hedonism, it is always clear within the context of Dennie's literary Federalism that mirth or merriment are given their real weight only when viewed in relation to what they oppose, the discontent of a monstrous human selfishness that, in all nations and ages, is the ultimate curse of the fallen world. Thus, for instance, a *Lay Preacher* on the Biblical text "What aileth thee?" is able to turn with no sense of discontinuity from moral psychology to politics: "What aileth thee, thou furious Jacobin? I know thy genius well. Though thy name, perhaps, is new, thy spirit is old. Thou didst not curse earth for the first time, during the decadence of the French monarchy. No, in the shape of Satan, thou didst crawl among the flowers of Eden . . . in the shape of Freedom didst thou banish order and comfort from mankind. . . . What has become of thy great archetype? Where is Robespierre and Marat and Condorcet?" (6:2:49–50).

In such a perspective as this, in which the uncontrolled power of the demos may be viewed as simply another of the ills brought into the world by Adam's sin, the murder and rapine of revolutionary upheaval bear much the same relation to the body politic as illness or disease to the physical body. This gives us the implicit logic through which the misery of Dennie's perpetual ill health, allegorized in the valetudinarianism of Oliver Oldschool, will expand to become in *The Port Folio* a metaphor for the miseries of American existence under Jeffersonian democracy. The same metaphor explains the symbolic importance given to those who respond to the vicissitudes of history with the cheerful indomitability as does Dennie to illness, as with the French nobleman who, having sustained three wounds in defense of his monarch against the revolutionary mob at the Tuileries, manages to escape alive: "Disguised in the habit of a groom," reports Oldschool in the *Farrago* recounting the Frenchman's story, "he reached the nearest port, and friendless, penniless, unknowing and unknown, he sought asylum in America" (1:66).

The pages of *The Port Folio* are full of French émigrés who have escaped the guillotine, survivors of the Terror who walk the streets of America as living reminders that the abstract doctrines of jacobin radicalism, so radiant in their proclaimed idealism of liberty and equality, have already acquired a real history of blood and human cruelty. Yet the French cavalier of this early *Farrago*, having seen more such history than any reader of *The Port Folio* is ever likely to see—"He has witnessed every rotation of fortune's wheel. He has seen the downfall of an hereditary monarch, a gallant nobility, and a venerated church"—will retain a special status because of what Oldschool calls his "gay philosophy," a virtual parable for Federalists in the age of Jefferson: "With inextinguishable vivacity, he recounts his own and his country's misfortunes, curses nothing but the club of Jacobins, and anticipates better days. Last night I heard him singing under an old elm 'Banissons la melancholie'" (1:66).

For Oliver Oldschool, whose own version of *"Banissons la melancholie"* has always been an escape into books and reading, it is the way literature serves to drive away thoughts of "the present pitiful politics of this country" (2:8), as he once puts it, that leads him gradually to identify his own ill health with the illness of America under Jeffersonian democracy. "When I meditate upon health, assailed by every sullen gale," says Dennie in "An Author's Evenings," but also "when I fall into . . . profound melancholy, as I meditate upon the degradation of my country," "I run to the merriest authors in my library" (2:410). It is in just the same spirit that we will hear him saying, several years later, that he has read *Don Quixote* ten times, for "a merrier work can scarcely be found, and because in the dull and dismal scenes of this wild world, a merry book doeth good like a medicine" (7:1:42).

The Port Folio's turn toward the aesthetic occurs as the gradual dawning of its awareness that escape into literature is itself a literary theme, that poetry and philosophy had almost from the beginning celebrated the power of language to create, in the midst of social misery or personal despair, other, happier worlds. The occasion on which Dennie speaks in so many words of a "philosophy of merriment" is, signifi-

58

cantly enough, in introducing into *The Port Folio* a Horatian imitation originally printed in *The Gentleman's Magazine* during the years of the North ministry, that low ebb of political fortunes in which England had been losing her American colonies and even such poets as Cowper and such statesmen as Burke had been wont to agree with their American brethren that Britain was a nation sunk in hopeless corruption. The Horace who is made to speak in English in *The Gentleman's Magazine*, and whose voice is then taken over by Dennie in *The Port Folio* in America's first year under Jefferson, is the poet who had himself sought refuge from the disorder of Roman political life in an ethic of *carpe diem:*

> Good friend, be calm, why should'st thou fret,
> Because the nation runs in debt,
> And taxes grow on taxes?
> . . . .
> I blush to hear a man complain
> That life expires too soon.
> What's life? A bubble of an hour;
> False as the wind; frail as the flower,
> And changeful as the moon.
> Why wilt thou then with boundless schemes,
> Disjointed as a sick man's dreams,
> Perplex thy bounded mind;
> And, grasping at the future hour,
> Let slip the present from thy power?
> Oh! impotent and blind!

Nowhere else in *The Port Folio*, perhaps, do we so clearly glimpse the close relationship that always exists in its pages between the *memento mori* theme and the philosophy of merriment, for which Dennie in this introductory headnote cites as his authorities, along with the Horace of the *carpe diem* odes, Epicurus in philosophy and Anacreon in Greek poetry. The Epicurus invoked at such moments is not, as Dennie points out in remarks made elsewhere, the hedonist of vulgar caricature. He is the sober philosopher of private retreat whose Garden stands as the first great exemplum of the otium ideal in classical thought. For it is this Epicurus, living in the seclusion of the Garden with a small community of friends, working out a doctrine of personal fulfillment in response to the decay of Athenian civic life and the decline of the Greek polis,[1] whose authority may be seen to lie behind the serious import even of Horace's more lighthearted *carpe diem* poetry, and, ultimately, *The Port Folio*'s own philosophy of merriment.

The far greater importance of Anacreon in *The Port Folio*'s symbolic universe, on the other hand, has to do with the Greek poet's discovery of an identical ethical or philosophical posture amidst the earliest disorders of Athenian democracy. "The heart of Anacreon," observes Oliver Oldschool in introducing an English translation of one of his odes, "devoted to indolence, seems to think that there is wealth enough in happiness, but seldom happiness enough in wealth" (4:72). The ode is a translation by Thomas Moore, whose own relation to *The Port Folio* and Dennie's literary circle may be taken as a virtual parable of the birth of a transatlantic republic of letters, with Moore initially heard as a distant voice speaking from the disembodied region of contemporary English poetry, then briefly and improbably materializing in America to become the convivial center of Dennie's literary circle in Philadelphia. After his Philadelphia sojourn, Moore is thus heard in *The Port Folio* not simply as the voice of Anacreontic values but of an emergent community of transatlantic souls sustained by those values in an otherwise shrunken and sordid age:

> But thus it is, all sects, we see,
> Have watch-words of morality;
> Some cry out Venus, others Jove,
> Here 'tis Religion, there 'tis Love!
> But while they thus so wisely wander,
> While mystics dream, and doctors ponder . . .
> The plain, good man, whose actions teach
> More virtue than a sect can preach,
> Pursues his course, unsagely blest,
> His tutor whispering in his breast. . . .
> (4:242)

The great lesson brought home to the *Port Folio* writers during Moore's visit to Philadelphia is that his own involvement with Anacreon, and in particular his sense that this neglected poet of Greek antiquity has something of importance to communicate to the present age, had been from the first a response on Moore's part to European history, a disenchantment with the world as it appears after the French Revolution and the rise of jacobin radicalism. This is the context in which Moore's response to Jeffersonian democracy, mirroring in transatlantic terms their own Federalist pessimism, will likewise bring home to Dennie and his circle that their warfare is not with Jefferson or his party but with modernity itself. "The ferment which the French revolution excited among the democrats of America," Moore will say in a book published after his return to England, echoing from across the Atlantic a constant theme of *The Port Folio*'s own verdict on Jeffersonian America, may be taken to explain "that hostility to all the graces of life, which distinguishes the present demagogues of the United States, and has become indeed too generally the characteristic of their countrymen" (6:2:153).[2]

By far the most important memorial of Moore's impact on *The Port Folio*, particularly as it points toward the logic of the magazine's subsequent shift towards a more purely Anacreontic posture, is James E. Hall's "Memoirs of Anacreon," serialized under Hall's usual *Port Folio* nom de plume "Sedley." For the "Memoirs" are the literary monument not simply of the impression made by Moore upon *The Port Folio* writers, but of certain truths, hidden before, that had come home to them only in conversation with him. "The design of this work," Hall will say at a later date when the "Memoirs" are being proposed for book publication, "was conceived during the transient visit Mr. Moore paid to this city in the summer of 1804. . . . It was communicated to Moore during one of those festive nights, which he has remembered in a manner not less honorable to himself than grateful to his friends. His approbation was expressed in a manner which was prompt, warm, and flattering" (7:1:48).

The truth brought home to the *Port Folio* writers by Moore's visit may be gathered from the project of imaginatively reconstructing around Anacreon's odes, from evidence in the poems themselves and from a more general knowledge of Greek antiquity, the sociocultural reality within which they might be assumed to have been produced. The general model for Hall's "Memoirs" is the *Voyage du jeune Anarcharsis en Grece* of the Abbé Barthelemy—Hall specifically cites "the ingenious plan of the Abbé Barthelemy" as his inspiration (7:1:248)—a hugely popular work, published just before the French Revolution, recounting the visit of an imaginary Syrian youth to the Greece of Epaminondas and Xenophon. Yet while this may suggest how widespread by the end of the eighteenth century had become the notion of "history" as a constructed or imagined reality, the "Memoirs" nonetheless represent an enterprise markedly different than Barthelemy's *Voyage*. For ancient Athens as re-created or reimagined in Hall's "Memoirs" is meant not simply to provide a setting for, but an explanation of, the odes of Anacreon.

The crucial truth about Anacreon's poetry of wine and love and laughter lies, in Hall's "Memoirs," in the world on which that poetry has resolutely turned its back, an Athenian democracy that had degenerated from mob rule into the tyranny of Pisistratus, who collected around himself, says "Sedley," "the base and the profligate, the needy and the designing, the restless and the ambitious, the ignorant and the credulous" (6:2:163). In the earlier years of *The Port Folio*, when Federalists like Dennie were still trying to understand the Jeffersonian ascendancy in classical republican terms, the historical parallel had an ominous implication: as degeneration into mob rule produced Pisistratus in Athens, it had produced Caesar in Rome and Cromwell in England and has now produced Napoleon in France, giving basis to the fear that uncontrolled democracy must in the United States lead to tyranny. The almost ruminative tone of Hall's "Memoirs of Anacreon," however, shows that the "demon of democracy" has now become a receding worry:

> Let the reader pause for a moment in this place, and reflect on the unvarying and detestable complexion which has always distinguished the features of this meretricious Siren. Let him view her folly and her profligacy in the streets of Athens . . . see her lighting the torch of discord, and blowing the trump of rebellion in England—and only furling her standard when it has been crimsoned by the blood of a sovereign;—and see her exhibit a still more hideous aspect, when she ravaged the fertile fields of France, imbrued her hands in the blood of a mild and benignant monarch, whose only crime was his love towards his subjects, and murdered thousands to satiate her savage ferocity; and at length plunged her deluded followers into the darkest gloom of despotism. Such is the demon of democracy. (6:2:184)

This is the message, by now so familiar to readers of *The Port Folio* as to constitute the virtual litany of its Federalism, that is in Hall's "Memoirs" unexpectedly put into an entirely new context by Anacreon's odes, which he quotes throughout in Moore's translation, and by the project of having to reconstruct through an effort of literary and historical imagination the society in which they were written. For the most important truth communicated by the "Memoirs" is ultimately implied by the very need to re-create around Anacreon's poems the reality about which they remain silent: as real as it seems, the teeming world of men and women that we ordinarily take to be so solid and actual is itself a dissolving reality in which nothing, including those men and women, is permanent or lasting. The one exception is art, and especially such arts of language as philosophy and history and poetry. Pisistratus and his followers have returned to dust, and the Athens in which they dwelt survives now only as a scattering of broken monuments, but the odes of Anacreon remain to greet other readers in other worlds.

The importance of *carpe diem* poetry for the *Port Folio* writers, in short, from Anacreon to Horace to the cavalier songs of Carew and Suckling to Tom Moore's own Anacreontic effusions in the present age, is that it brings to light the meaning of the aesthetic in a world given over to mutability and decay. "What's life?" we have heard an English Horace say: "The bubble of an hour." Yet the poetry that asks this question, and always answers it this way, is not the bubble of an hour. It is the great denier of its own dire mutterings about the impermanence of all that belongs to human existence, about marble tombs and fallen petals and deserts of vast eternity. In every age of poetry, perhaps, the deeper meaning of the *carpe diem* mode lies in this implicit and paradoxical celebration of poetry's own permanence in a world of death and loss, but only at certain moments in history is it given to readers to gaze through the inconsequentiality of its paeans to wine and laughter to a deeper truth about the timelessness of aesthetic experience.

The notion of the aesthetic as a separate and timeless realm appears with such suddenness in *The Port Folio*, and then in such obvious association with Anacreon and Moore and the magazine's subsequent Anacreontic posture, that it is tempting to see it as being due to Moore's dramatic appearance in Philadelphia at just the moment Dennie and his contributors had reached a low point of Federalist disillusionment. Yet Moore's visit did no more than crystallize certain values and assumptions already implicit in *The Port Folio*'s earlier conception of literature. Thus, for instance, we may hear Dennie in one of the magazine's earliest issues railing humorously at those devotees of "practical" education who make special claims for mathematics as mental training, and through this raillery mounting a serious counterclaim about literary reality: "Any object, that engrosses the mind, will induce a habit of attention. . . . a description from Virgil, a scene from Shakespeare . . . or any striking passage from authors of polite literature, will accomplish this purpose. Why should the demonstrations of Euclid arrogate this honor solely to themselves?" (1:110).

To take seriously the idea of literature as a timeless reality, of Aeneas or Hamlet or Falstaff as dwelling in the same realm of immateriality as prime numbers or Euclidean figures, is to see that this, even more than the notion of laughter or diversion, has from the beginning made reading so central to *The Port Folio*'s philosophy of merriment. "In this languid season of the natural year," says Dennie early in 1802, "and in this gloomy season of the political one, I . . . strive to lose, or at least to mitigate my sense of the tyranny of the American populace, by reading merry books"; "I sit up all night," he will say a bit later, "to read FIELDING AND RABELAIS." And then, as sometimes happens, we get a glimpse of the way literature as a separate reality makes real this possibility of reading as diversion. In Horace, says Dennie, we hear of that man whose characteristic was that he *risus undique quaerit:* "This seeker of mirth was a wise man; and while we are restrained in this 'prison-house the world,' it is the most judicious part to look as smilingly as we can from our grate" (2:213).

The Port Folio's retreat from history, though it will be proclaimed as such only when the magazine formally renounces politics in 1809, thus originates in all those earlier moments when Oliver Oldschool and his contributors are moved by events to cultivate the notion of literature as a separate reality. The birth of literary Federalism occurs in *The Port Folio* as its writers begin consciously to collaborate in the project of creating an imaginary world in opposition to the actual society of Jeffersonian America. For the truth that comes home to Dennie and the *Port Folio* writers is that the degeneration into democratic rule in America is not, after all, going to end in the tyranny of a Pisistratus or a Napoleon. The American tyranny will be that of a demos motivated solely by material pursuits and given the means to perpetuate its own existence through a new ideology of the common man. This is literary Federalism as one begins to hear its voice in, for instance, an extract reprinted in *The Port Folio* in 1805 from *The Companion*, a new paper published in Baltimore, whose editor specifically bans from his readership those "who are immersed in business, whose souls are exclusively devoted to the pursuit of riches, who suffer no ideas to intrude upon their speculations, or to disturb their calculations on exchange, insurance, and bank stock" (5:60).

In *The Port Folio*, the Anacreontic posture of mirth or merriment will normally be represented as what might be called a principled indolence, a determination, in an America increasingly driven by business and commerce and the frantic pursuit of riches, to lounge through life devoting oneself to company and conversation and good books. This is again something that originates with Dennie himself, whose early stylizations of his own personality provide the cues for nearly everything that later happens in *The Port Folio* as a whole. Thus, for instance, Dennie had reprinted in an early *Port Folio* several numbers of *The Farrago* devoted to Menander, a young lawyer bewitched by polite literature, which every reader was expected to understand as Dennie's self-portrait: "So entirely devoted is he to the cultivation of the belles lettres, that his graver moments, instead of being devoted to Blackstone and Buller, are given to Shakespeare and Sterne. He reads plays when he should be filling writs; and the other day, attempting to draw a deed, instead of 'Know all men by these presents,' he scribbled a simile from Spenser" (1:30).

In biographical terms, the Menander essays look back to Dennie's legal apprenticeship in New Hampshire, the days when, as a young Harvard graduate, he had briefly tried the law before gravitating toward the editorship of the *Farmer's Museum*. Yet the Menander portrait even in those earlier days belonged more to literary tradition than to Dennie's actual life in Walpole, and in particular to the comic tradition of the Inner Temple law student who, in eighteenth-century England, had become notorious as a cultural stereotype by neglecting the law and setting up instead as a coffeehouse critic, holding forth at White's or Will's on the merits or demerits of a new play or a recently published poem. Menander belongs, in short, less to Walpole or Philadelphia than to the London of *The Tatler* and *The Spectator* and Dr. Johnson's Dick Minim, and Dennie's *Farragos* are meant to assert a vital relation between that world and the world of *The Lay Preacher* and, subsequently, Oliver Oldschool and *The Port Folio*.

The importance of Menander's world in *The Port Folio* will be precisely that it is a literary place, not simply because it takes what Dennie calls belles lettres or polite literature as the center of its own values, but because it is constructed out of literature as an imaginary reality belonging in equal measure to readers on either side of the Atlantic, to all those souls as much at home inside the pages of *The Spectator*, the world of Will Honeycomb and Sir Roger de Coverley, as in the actual streets of London or Walpole, New Hampshire. The numbers of *The Farrago* given over to Menander's journal are, besides being good-humored self-mockery on Dennie's part, the assertion of a serious system of values:

Tuesday.—Overslept myself, did not rise till nine. Dressed, and went out, intending to go to the office; but, as the morning was uncommonly beautiful, I recollected an aphorism of Dr. Cheyne's, that exercise should form part of a student's religion. Accordingly, I rambled through the woods for two hours. The magic of rural scenes diverted Fancy, whom, on my return to the office, I wished to retire, that her elder sister, Judgment, might have an opportunity to hold a conference with the sage Blackstone: but, the sportive slut remained, dancing about, and I found my spirits so agitated, that, to calm them, I took up a volume of plays, and read two acts in Centlivre's Busy Body. (1:30)

Beneath the gentle self-mockery of such passages, readers of *The Port Folio* were expected to glimpse a serious relation to the classical ideal of otium, to understand that a life devoted to Shakespeare and Sterne and Spenser's *Faerie Queene* represents, in a country looking to nothing higher than the pursuit of soul-destroying dollars, a kind of moral parable. The task of representing this viewpoint in *The Port Folio* belongs to *The American Lounger*, an imitation of Henry Mackenzie's Edinburgh periodical *The Lounger* written by various members of Dennie's circle under the nom de plume Samuel Saunter, Esq. In a society dominated by economic self-interest, lounging assumes a burden of serious moral implication precisely because it so openly violates the maxims of self-interest. The ongoing irony in *The American Lounger* lies in the way its own celebrations of indolence imply contempt for an America in which reading itself is largely regarded as a waste of time. "To that laziness which the body assumes, out of complaisance to the understanding," writes one "Spencer" to Samuel Saunter, "I shall ever pay a sincere, though it be a secret homage. . . . I have seen nothing disgraceful in that mental abandonment of Thomson and Shenstone, which the woolen-drapers of their day called indolence" (2:81).

As *The Port Folio* turns its back more and more on contemporary American politics, the inevitable tendency of *The American Lounger* and the other periodical series that begin to appear in the pages of the magazine—*The Recluse, The Polite Scholar, The Beehive, The Salad*, etc.—is to redirect the gaze of the magazine as a whole towards England and Europe, or rather towards an English and European literary tradition that has come to seem the only remaining sanctuary of the spirit in Jeffersonian America, and at the same time towards a past which, belonging partly to America and partly to Europe and existing now only in the imagination, offers a similar refuge from a degraded present. Thus it is, for instance, that a correspondent addressing himself to *The American Lounger* will spontaneously identify Samuel Saunter with a line of essayists writing not in America but in Britain—"The Tatler, Spectator, Guardian, Adventurer, Rambler, Idler, World, Connoisseur, Observer, Mirror and Lounger" (3:401)—as though imagining both Saunter and himself as dwellers in a reality that, beyond the accidents of time and nation, had some time since become wholly literary.

The great model of politesse in this situation is the modern version of Aristippus who enters the pages of *The Port Folio* in the poetry of John Gilbert Cooper, with whom Dennie goes out of the way to identify his Lay Preacher persona. This is the model of urbanity, its remote origins lying in the Spectatorial posture of Addison and Steele toward early-eighteenth-century English society, that in the later years of Dennie's editorship will come to occupy the literary center of *The Port Folio*, with such series as *The Beehive* or *The Salad*, or Dennie himself as heard in such departments as "An Author's Evenings," projecting outward the idea of an audience of polite readers whose own world of wit and civility becomes the central image of the magazine. Though reminders of a rougher and more boisterous Jeffersonian reality will intrude themselves into *The Port Folio* right up to the end, they are after a certain point registered as though through a protective medium of civilized consciousness, as the tumult of a drunken crowd might distantly be heard from within a drawing room in which the fire blazes and tea is being served. This is the world of those for whom *The Spectator* and *The Rambler* and *The Life of Johnson* have grown more real than Jefferson and Duane and *The Aurora*.

The point at which *The American Lounger* is joined in *The Port Folio* by such periodical series as *The Polite Scholar* and *The Beehive* may on the same account be taken to mark a final transmutation of the magazine's philosophy of merriment into a determination to produce through literary means, as *The Spectator* had once transformed English society and *The Lounger* that of Scotland, an alternative community able to insulate itself from Jeffersonian America. This is the spirit in which Dennie enthusiastically welcomes *Salmagundi*, the work of Washington Irving and his circle in New York, as a partner in the enterprise of literary Federalism: "A work has lately been published in New York, entitled Salmagundi. . . . It bears the stamp of superior genius, and indicates its unknown authors to be possessed of lively and vigorous imaginations, a happy turn for ridicule, and an extensive knowledge of the world. Like the Spectator, its design is to mend the morals, correct the manners, and improve the taste of the age" (7:1:179).

As has long been recognized, the *Salmagundi* authors in New York understood themselves to be the counterpart of the *Port Folio* circle in Philadelphia, just as Washington Irving's Jonathan Oldstyle persona, already familiar to New York readers from Irving's essays in *The Morning Chronicle*, had been meant to announce his literary kinship with Dennie's Oliver Oldschool. What has not been remarked is that the appearance of *Salmagundi*, joining *The Port Folio* in its separate world of wit and fancy, content to signal its distance from Jeffersonian America through satire or ridicule, marks the birth of literary Federalism as such.[3] Thus Dennie, reprinting in *The Port Folio* a recent essay by Irving—"a well principled Federalist," Dennie calls him—is able to describe *Salmagundi* in terms that virtually announce the existence of a separate, secret, literary world: "Its avowed object is . . . to deride the follies of fashion, and to expose the absurdity of our institutions. Its editors are a confederacy of men of wit and men of the world; and though they have very carefully concealed themselves from the public, they are not unknown to us" (7:1:308).

In the middle years of Dennie's editorship, the philosophy of merriment that had begun in Oliver Oldschool's cheerfulness in the face of illness, expanding then under Moore's inspiration into an Anacreontic turning away from the miseries of democracy, thus becomes a mode of literary warfare against the mental inertness of a nation given over entirely to the pursuit of material gain. "It has been remarked," says Dennie in 1809, ". . . that the national character is phlegmatic, and that the Powers of Merriment, Wit, and Humor, are strangled, by the iron hand of care, or at least checked by the severity of business" (9:1:94). "Much is written and published here," he had complained a year earlier, "but principally of an exceedingly grave cast. Our literature has as long and woeful a visage as many of those Puritans" from whom Americans are descended: "A great majority of the elaborate essays of our Columbian composuists . . . would exactly suit the taste of Praise-God-Barebones" (8:2:280).

The visage of Jeffersonian democracy as seen in *The Port Folio* subsequent to the magazine's renunciation of politics will almost always be some version of that of Praise God Barebones as he appears here. Yet this is the Puritan not so much as religious fanatic as humorless philistine, the representative of a nation endlessly complacent in its own narrow-mindedness and ignorance, endlessly proud of its devotion to the commonness of the common man. This is that tyranny of mindlessness against which *The Port Folio* will go on waging spiritual warfare in the name of mirth and merriment—"even in America," Dennie will hope from time to time, "a Rabelais, a Sterne, or a Gay might be found" (9:1:94)— but it is also a reality from which it will at the same time increasingly seek refuge in an alternative world of literature and language and cultural memory, a republic of letters from which the democratic demagogues and ragged backwoodsmen of Jeffersonian America are blessedly absent, and in which the wiser citizens of every age and nation are equally at home.

Chapter Four

The Republic of Letters

IN July 1810 *The Port Folio* introduced *The Beehive*, a new periodical series whose inaugural essay celebrated literature as a "sanctum sanctorum," a refuge for the mind or spirit in a country "where party passions too frequently reign uncontrolled." The notion of literature as a sanctuary from the tumults and contentions of public life, says *The Beehive* writer, implies nothing less than "the elements of a code of laws for the government of the republic of letters" in America (10:2:66).[1] Whenever *The Port Folio* speaks of a republic of letters in the later years of Dennie's editorship, it is normally in this sense of a domain of thought or imagination separate from ordinary American life, both at the individual level of ceaseless economic striving—"The spirit of this country is so truly mercantile," James E. Hall laments in his "Memoirs of Anacreon," "that no pursuit is regarded, which has not wealth for its object" (8:1:36)—and at the civic level on which Jeffersonian ideology has been promoted, latterly with resounding success, as the civic ideology of America.

As we have seen, the Federalist republic of letters is to a great extent born from the demise of the classical republican vision in the sphere of actual politics. "Our fond notions of the superior virtue and information of our countrymen," one *Port Folio* writer gloomily confesses in the second term of Jefferson's presidency, "we find to be but waking dreams" (7:1:380). It is the sense of having been marooned inside a waking dream that explains *The Port Folio's* growing isolation or estrangement from an America now more and more driven by raw economic individualism. In Jeffersonian America, the author of an "Hours of Leisure" essay will say, "a few selfish and contracted ideas constitute the mind of man, who becomes a species of clock-work, a machine, or automaton of the particular occupation which he fills. Business and money form his providence" (7:2:202). This is the runaway engine of a new money or market society as it careens towards the terminus of a now-unfathomable history, leaving behind a small company of Federalist souls stranded within an increasingly unreal world of classical republican assumptions.

The Port Folio had formally renounced politics in favor of literary and cultural subjects at the beginning of 1809. The great paradox is that the magazine at this moment of renunciation does not become the mere ghostly voice of a remembered Federalism, the weak or dying echo of a world that, having lost its battle for legitimation in the realm of the actual, fades to become another curiosity in the museum of vanished mythologies and defunct cultural systems. To the contrary, the moment that Oliver Oldschool announces *The Port Folio*'s turn away from politics marks the beginning of what is in its way a new lease on life for the magazine, a period during which its sense of its own reality will be altogether as robust as during the long years of its opposition to jacobinism and Jefferson. During this period, which is brought to a sudden unexpected close only by the untimely death of Joseph Dennie, the republic of letters will become for *The Port Folio* and its audience more real or substantial than the alienated and fragmented world of American democracy.

The paradox is resolved, it seems to me, when we see that *The Port Folio*'s own conception of the republic of letters represents a special and problematic instance of what Habermas has taught us to think of as the public sphere, that "world of a critically debating reading public" (Habermas 106) created in the seventeenth and eighteenth centuries by print technology and the growth of European literacy, a disembodied realm of opinion separate at once from the private life of individuals and the public life of the nation in the traditional sense of legislation or government. For the renewal of energy that occurs when *The Port Folio* turns away from politics derives from its unexpected discovery that classical republican values—*virtus*, literature or learning as ends in themselves, the possibility of a genuine aristocracy of mind or intellect—have unaccountably been granted a right of survival in a realm made possible by a modern system of publication and communication.

Yet on any conventional understanding of Federalism, the modernity of the system ought to present a major problem. For it is precisely because the public sphere is a modern phenomenon that Habermas is led to associate it with just the forces of Enlightenment skepticism and militant rationalism against which *The Port Folio* had in its earlier years waged such unremitting war. The real discoverer of the public sphere, on Habermas's account, is Kant, who had seen very clearly, even as it was still happening around him, that the world had been altered in a certain significant way by the widespread availability of printed texts and a vast anonymous reading public. What Kant understood is that it was the anonymity of the new public that mattered: the educated Roman reading Greek philosophy or the medieval Christian reading Virgil had not been doing anything essentially different from the eighteenth-century reader of Hume or Voltaire or Diderot. What is new, as Kant says in a famous section of *Was ist Aufklarung?*, is that writers in the modern age begin to write with a full consciousness of putting themselves "before the reading public" (qtd. in Habermas 106). From this arises the possibility of an abstract *opinion publique* increasingly able to moderate or regulate the doings of princes and parliaments.

For Habermas, therefore, the significance of the new public sphere lies in the way it permits the free exercise of critical reason in the impersonal domain of the printed word. This same notion of a certain essential relation between the public sphere and "progressive" history is retained in *The Letters of the Republic*, Michael Warner's study of the American Revolution as an event in some sense produced by print culture. On Warner's account, what creates the modern public sphere is not the mere spread of print technology or citizen literacy but, at a certain critical point, a momentous alteration in the very epistemology of reading. The public sphere is what springs into existence when people begin to read with a full consciousness that they dwell in a world of readers, when one gazes upon the page with a simultaneous awareness that this text is available on identical terms to innumerable other human minds—when the reader, as Warner himself puts it, "incorporates into the meaning of the printed object an awareness of the potentially limitless others who may also be reading" (xiii).

The great virtue of Warner's account is that it permits one immediately to understand how *The Port Folio*, beginning from an essentially Habermasian conception of the public sphere, could then nonetheless come to see the new print culture as dangerous or harmful to civic values. For in the modern age, the Federalist writers saw, a reader does not simply gaze upon the printed page subliminally aware that it is simultaneously available to millions of other readers, but also with a sense of those others as existing now, at one's own moment in history. The great danger posed by democratic print culture is that it projects the public sphere in a way that permits the demos to dwell in a perpetual present—in a way that, indeed, makes the tendency to dwell in such a present, driven only by goals and gratifications relating to the short span of individual existence, the virtual definition of what it means to belong to the demos. For *The Port Folio*, this is sufficient to explain the ascendancy in Jeffersonian America of papers like Duane's *Aurora* and the "democratic republican" press generally.

71

At the root of *The Port Folio*'s antipathy towards the Jeffersonian press lies an even deeper anxiety, however, which is that the modern system of publication has become a sort of machine for producing the demos as what Benedict Anderson has called an "imagined community floating in homogeneous, empty time" (116). Anderson's subject in *Imagined Communities*, the superb study whose theoretical analysis Warner so suggestively extends to the early American republic, is the role of literacy and print culture in creating the twentieth-century postcolonial state. Yet only a small effort of imagination is needed to transpose into Federalist terms Anderson's description of modern newspaper consumption as a sort of ritual or ceremony:

> The obsolescence of the newspaper on the morrow of its printing . . . creates this extraordinary mass ceremony: the almost precisely simultaneous consumption ("imagining") of the newspaper-as-fiction. . . . The significance of this mass ceremony is paradoxical. It is performed in silent privacy, in the lair of the skull. Yet each communicant is well aware that the ceremony he performs is being replicated simultaneously by thousands (or millions) of others of whose existence he is confident, yet of whose identity he has not the slightest notion. . . . What more vivid figure for the secular, historically clocked, imagined community can be envisioned? At the same time, the newspaper reader, observing exact replicas of his own paper being consumed by his subway, barbershop, or residential neighbors, is continually reassured that the imagined world is visibly rooted in everyday life. (35)

The paradox is thus that *The Port Folio* is somehow able to accept modern print culture as the most fundamental condition of its own existence, looking back without apparent anxiety on its own descent from such Enlightenment periodicals as Bayle's *Nouvelles de la Republique des Lettres*, listing the foreign and domestic publications with which it maintains a network of communication, pausing not infrequently to discuss the history of printing and its effects on modern consciousness. Thus Dennie will take from the French of La Harpe, for instance, an account of "the memorable epoch of the invention of printing" that might today stand as an epigraph to Eisenstein or Habermas: "by multiplying with the greatest facility the images of thought, there is established, from one end of the world to the other, a continual and speedy correspondence of reason and genius" (6:1:6). Or, in the same vein, another *Port Folio* writer's unsentimental farewell to the ancient ideal of eloquence:

Oral eloquence, as displayed in public harangues, is . . . of much less value to the public, than the eloquence of written composition. It serves indeed many temporary and valuable purposes, promotes private interest, raises friends, fortune, characters, and is therefore greatly to be esteemed, and studiously cultivated; but, after all, it is not, since books have abounded, indispensably essential to the welfare of society, nor absolutely necessary to the improvement of human nature. These grand purposes may be more effectually and more extensively accomplished by the able writer.[2]

For such writers as this, obviously, it is the existence of *The Port Folio* itself that resolves the paradox. The modernity of the new print culture presents no terrors for a *Port Folio* contributor precisely because *The Port Folio* has demonstrated, simply by existing and having a loyal readership, that the public sphere is, after all, an abstract system of social and technological relations with no ideological content of its own. So while it is true that in the modern age *The Aurora* and other Jeffersonian newspapers crowd the public sphere, it is also true that a reader opening *The Port Folio* may turn away from the world of *The Aurora* to enter a Federalist republic of letters sustained by the vision of traditional or organic society lying at the heart of classical republican thought. For Oliver Oldschool and the *Port Folio* writers, whose actuality is the raw and sprawling vigor of an America irreversibly given over to Jeffersonian democracy, the more momentous truth that now dawns is that history as experienced by their fellow citizens, that eternal present of the demos in which one reads *The Aurora* and pursues the way to wealth unaware that there were human civilizations before one's own, is in comparison with this remembered organic society illusory or unreal.

The Port Folio's retreat from politics may be said to begin in its growing sense that the demos, created after all not by Jefferson or democracy but by a deeper social transformation, has become irrevocably cut off from any living relation to the cultural past. *The Port Folio*'s lack of anxiety about its own relation to the modern world of print and publication derives, on the other hand, from its gradual discovery that the same public sphere that sustains the demos in its perpetual present has in an altogether unexpected way become a last refuge or sanctuary for readers who have remained true to classical republican values. This is the truth that dawns during the period that Burke's voice begins to be heard with increasing resonance in *The Port Folio*, and when Tom Moore's visit to Philadelphia is spontaneously taken by Dennie and his circle to mark an epoch in literary Federalism, a moment when certain scattered souls on both sides of the Atlantic begin to see that they have more in common with one another than with members of their own societies whose minds have been seduced by jacobinism and democracy.

The Port Folio is led to this conclusion through its own steady insistence on an alternative ontology of reading—an idea of literature as existing outside historical time—whose roots in classical republican thought go back to the Stoic wisdom of ancient Greece and Rome. "No age is forbidden us," Seneca had said about reading in the *Epistulae Morales:* "There is a vast stretch of time for us to roam. We may dispute with Socrates, . . . repose with Epicurus. . . . Why should we not take ourselves in mind from this petty and ephemeral span to the boundless and timeless region we can share with our betters?" (65–70). To envision literature as a source of timeless truth or wisdom, as Federalist writing invariably does, is thus to insist on language as the logos or principle of transcendent rationality shared by human consciousness and the universe in every age and culture. "Literature is the gift of Heaven," says a Federalist writer quoted in *The Port Folio* from *The Troy Gazette,* "a ray of that wisdom which governs the universe; and which man, inspired by celestial intelligence, has drawn down to earth. . . . By the aid of literature, we bring around us all things, all places, men, and times."[3]

This is the classical republican theory of reading in its purest form, an ethical vision that completes and renders substantial the idea of a Federalist republic of letters. For up to a certain critical point, as we have seen, the notion of literature as a separate sphere is dominated in *The Port Folio* simply by the increasingly felt need to escape unpleasant reality, giving us in the first instance Oliver Oldschool's philosophy of merriment and later, after Moore's visit to America, the Anacreontic posture of the magazine towards Jeffersonian democracy. It is the vision of reading as entry not merely to a separate but to a superior order of reality, a place where one converses with Socrates and Cicero, that then bestows reality upon the Federalist idea of literature as a world elsewhere. "In many of the old romances," says Dennie in a late *Lay Preacher,*

we are gravely informed, that the unfortunate knight in the dungeon of some giant, or fascinated by some witch or enchanter, while he sees nothing but hideousness and horror before him, if haply a fairy, or some other benignant being, impart a talisman of wondrous virtue, on a sudden our disconsolate prisoner finds himself in a magnificent palace, or a beautiful garden, in the bower of Beauty, or in the arms of Love. This wild fable, which abounds in the legends of knight-errantry, has always appeared to me very finely to shadow out the enchantment of study. A book produces a delightful abstraction from the cares and sorrows of this world. They may press upon us, but when we are engrossed by study we do not very acutely feel them. Nay, by the magic illusion of a fascinating author we are transported from the couch of Anguish, or the grip of Indigence to Milton's Paradise or the Elysium of Virgil. (8:1:50)

By the time the Lay Preacher utters these words, *The Port Folio* will have long since sought its own spiritual home in the imaginary English society, itself sustained by a strong sense of the classical past, that lives on in the works of the eighteenth-century Augustan writers: Pope and Swift and Bolingbroke as they had fought a long literary warfare against Walpole and modernity, Goldsmith and Johnson and Burke as these had then sought to preserve a sense of Augustan values in a fragmenting and declining world. Dennie's own sense of Augustan England as his own real spiritual home explains the preponderance of eighteenth-century writers—Pope, Bolingbroke, Addison, Johnson, Burke—in his account of the alternative society made available by reading. The studious man, says Dennie, meaning by implication the Federalist reader, "may visit Pliny at his villa, or Pope at Twickenham. . . . He may make philosophical experiments with Bacon, or enjoy the eloquence of Bolingbroke. He may speculate with Addison, moralize with Johnson, read tragedies and comedies with Shakespeare, and be raptured by the rhetoric of Burke" (8:1:50).

The great attraction of Augustan England for Dennie and the *Port Folio* writers is that they are able to recognize in Pope's Horatian poems or Bolingbroke's *Idea of a Patriot King* or Goldsmith's *The Deserted Village* an imaginative world sustained, in the midst of political disorder and religious skepticism and the disintegrative energies of a new market economy, by the memory of a traditional or organic society in which life had yet seemed spiritually coherent and whole. Thus Pope, for instance, is for *The Port Folio* preeminently the poet of Twickenham, living in otium retirement from the brawl and clamor of Walpole's England, and thus Samuel Johnson, in the next age, becomes the hero of an orthodoxy maintained in defiance of modern skepticism and unbelief. "The single weight of Johnson's massy understanding, in the scale of Christianity," says one of his American admirers in *The Port Folio*, "is an overbalance to all the infidelity of the age, in which he lived."[4]

The image of Augustan England so dominates *The Port Folio* that an intimate knowledge of *The Spectator* or Pope's poetry or Boswell's *Life of Johnson* is simply and silently assumed in the conversation between Oliver Oldschool and his readers. By the middle period of Dennie's editorship, the world of Johnson and Burke and Garrick, the Turk's Head and Drury Lane and *The Gentleman's Magazine*, has in a certain important sense become more real to *The Port Folio* and its audience than Jeffersonian America. Yet it is not the gigantic figures of Burke or Johnson who preside symbolically over *The Port Folio*'s withdrawal into the sphere of late Augustan reality. That role is reserved for Oliver Goldsmith, who had himself been an outsider and even a misfit in the literary world of Johnson's England, an Irishman of shadowy antecedents, an awkward conversationalist and occasional butt of wit, a poverty-stricken Grub Street hack.

The role of Goldsmith as the tutelary spirit of literary Federalism originates in Dennie's own strong sense, dating from his Walpole days and even before, of being himself an outsider in a society that cares nothing about literature or learning, where "the best and brightest" minds, as he once says in implicitly comparing his own case in America to Goldsmith's early literary obscurity in Ireland, are overwhelmed by the forces of "stupidity, avarice, or faction." This is Dennie as he will always see in Goldsmith's career a mirror of his own circumstances and aspirations, though it is never clear that Dennie imagines that even Goldsmith could have achieved literary success under the conditions of Jeffersonian democracy. "Suppose Goldsmith in a region," says Dennie bitterly, knowing full well that *Port Folio* readers will understand him to be talking about himself, where "he was jostled by atheists, deists, new philosophers, jacobins, convicts, swindlers, peddlers, speculators, horse jockies . . . and buffoons" (3:93).

The Goldsmith meant to be honored when Dennie chooses Oliver Oldschool as a name for his own editorial persona is not simply the writer who had begun in obscurity and ended in fame—from Horace to Ben Jonson, as Dennie was wholly aware, literary history does not lack for such examples—but who had done so specifically within the new world of modern print culture and the public sphere, in this a more pure example, given his Irishness and outsider status, than even his great friend and patron Samuel Johnson. This is the Goldsmith who on the level of purely economic survival had been compelled to maintain himself through periodical writing and translation and historical compilation, *The Bee* and *The History of Animated Nature* and contributions to *The British Magazine* and *Critical Review*, but who nonetheless on the literary or intellectual level had succeeded in creating a luminous world of benevolent good nature, of gentle wit and generous piety and moral simplicity, seeming to exist magically apart from the conditions of modernity.

Whenever *The Port Folio* posits Goldsmith's writing as a model or ideal, it tends to do so in terms of style, using terms—ease, naturalness, simplicity, vivacity—that we should now be inclined to associate with "voice." Yet when Dennie recommends Goldsmith as an example to young writers, it is clear that he sees as the deeper source of such stylistic qualities Goldsmith's unwavering vision of an older, simpler, more virtuous society. Thus, for instance, the passage taken by Dennie from *The Vicar of Wakefield* ostensibly to demonstrate the superiority of Goldsmith's style will be, not coincidentally, a picture of traditional English village life already receding into memory: "remote from the polite, they still retained a primeval simplicity of manners, and, frugal by long habit, scarcely knew that temperance was a virtue. They wrought with cheerfulness on days of labour, but observed festivals as intervals of idleness. They kept up the Christmas carol; sent true love knots on Valentine morning; . . . showed their wit on the first of April; and religiously cracked nuts on Michaelmas eve" (1:28).

As it survives in *The Deserted Village*, with its deep mourning for a traditional order engulfed by new money or market forces, Goldsmith's vision of organic society represents a last urgent critique of modernity, and an element of that critical spirit registers even when, as here in *The Vicar of Wakefield*, the same vision has begun to serve as an imaginative refuge from the modern age. This spirit will remain when literary Federalism, under the inspiration of Goldsmith's writing, begins to turn its gaze towards an older English or European past in which feudal relations symbolize the ancient ties of mutual rights and responsibilities that had once bound together men and women in genuine community. Thus, for instance, the account of a young Scots nobleman's coming-of-age celebration taken by *The Port Folio* from a British publication:

The day was announced by the ringing of bells at the neighboring churches. . . . In the evening there was a brilliant display of fireworks, and bonfires were raised on every hill and every farm on the estate, to evince the attachment to the proprietor, and joy which the inhabitants felt on the occasion of this amiable young nobleman's succeeding to his extensive property. . . . The tenants danced to the Scotch bagpipes, and continued in the highest glee till seven the next morning. . . . The scene brought to mind the festivity of ancient days, and will, no doubt, be a theme of grateful recollection for many a year to those who witnessed it. (6:1:27)

The Port Folio's tendency to idealize such scenes, together with its evident tendency to dwell imaginatively in Augustan England in preference to Jeffersonian America, is the basis of those "English sympathies" and "aristocratical leanings" denounced by Duane's *Aurora* as unrepublican and, perhaps worse, un-American. Yet their obvious function for a literary Federalism increasingly alienated from actual history is to serve as a moral measure of what is being lost in an American society dominated by economic individualism, an explanation of why souls yet mindful of an older classical republican vision of society should feel that there is something degraded about this new world of swindlers, speculators, horse jockeys, and buffoons. This is a point so obvious to Dennie that he can only respond with a mixture of outrage and bafflement to the charge that he is, in being critical of Jefferson's America, himself somehow not American,[5] but it was one that would permanently elude Duane and the democratic republican press.

The nightmare vision of an America mindlessly driven by material pursuits, which emerges most powerfully in *The Port Folio* precisely during this later period of its exile from politics, would survive as one of its major legacies to later American thought and writing. "Why should we live with such hurry and waste of life?" Thoreau will memorably ask in *Walden*, summing up American life in the image of an epileptic or nervous seizure: "We have the St. Vitus dance, and cannot possibly keep our heads still." Yet this had been precisely the verdict of literary Federalism nearly half a century before. An American wishing to save his soul or his sanity, says the author of *The Recluse*, a series published in *The Port Folio* in the last year of Dennie's editorship, must leave society and retire to the woods, for it is "to be diseased with St. Vitus's dance, with a vengeance, if he must continue to dance on, rain or shine, contrary to his own inclination!" (11:1:297).

In a number of ways, and not least as the last great expression of the otium ideal in English, Thoreau's *Walden* may be read as the moral voice of literary Federalism returning to utterance after a long apparent silence. Yet the silence has only been apparent, for though literary Federalism had in an important sense gone into exile with Washington Irving's long sojourn in Europe—the Irving of such "English" works as *Bracebridge Hall* and the books about Spain—it is also true that the values giving point to *Walden*'s uncompromising critique of American society will have been preserved by the earlier withdrawal of Dennie and the *Port Folio* writers from any direct engagement with Jeffersonian democracy. For that disengagement had been meant to raise in insistent terms the otium paradox, as old as Epicurus and the community of the Garden, that a decision to retire from the world is always in some silent or unenunciated sense the severest of moral judgments on the world.

The way *The Port Folio* insists on this perspective is to surround its own withdrawal from politics with reminders of the otium tradition, a process that begins long before the magazine's announcement in 1809 that it will have no more to do with "squabbles in the State," and that then becomes altogether unmistakable in the proliferation of writing on otium themes—rural retirement, literary leisure, classical reading, books as the treasure of the mind—that comes to dominate its pages. This is the sense in which Oliver Oldschool's renunciation of politics in 1809 will have been long since anticipated, even allegorized, five years before in a remarkable *American Lounger* in which one Rusticus, visited by an old college friend, defends at length his reasons for turning his back on Jeffersonian America—"the fiends and demons," as he phrases it, "who enchant, and pollute our land"— and dwelling entirely within the boundaries of his country estate:

My farm, supplies me with all the necessaries, and many of the comforts of life. I can afford to open a bottle of wine, on those rare occasions, like the present, when a friend honors me with a call, and we talk over the tale of other times, and renew the memory of joys, that are past. I find leisure on Sunday, to sit, or slumber, *sub antiqua ilice*, and there I peruse *The Port Folio*, and indulge in a luxury which Horace never knew . . . a pipe of good tobacco. Shall I then abandon these comforts, to follow the will O wisp ambition? For what purpose? To gain either power or fame? As to the first, to a man of my sentiments, and in a government like ours, it is unattainable. I who may truly say, *odi profanum vulgus*, and who entertain a sovereign contempt for the *civium ardor prava jubentium* shall I have the folly, to hope for the applauses, or the votes of the rabble—it would be as wise to attempt climbing a thorn locust. (4:305)

This is the voice of literary Federalism as it will be heard in *The Port Folio* throughout the last years of Dennie's editorship, the voice of a community that has renounced the world in favor of a republic of letters existing now only in books and the cultural memory of those devoted to them. It is books, says the author of *The Polite Scholar*, another of those periodical series initiated in *The Port Folio* in this latter period, that have drawn him away "from all the pursuits of avarice or ambition": "I never yet pulled off my hat to the populace for the sake of their suffrages to office, nor would I run to the Indies, like the merchant in Horace. . . . Content in my cloister, with a few favorite authors, and still fewer dots and ducats, I strive to make a liberal economy supply the want of treasure, and explore my mines of treasure, in the Bible, Milton, and Cowper" (10:2:81). No clearer statement could be sought of the way the Federalist retreat from history has come to rest in literature as a world elsewhere.

During Dennie's last years as editor, *The Port Folio* operates as a mirror held up to the American society from which it has in formal terms disengaged, giving back by way of reverse or positive image, with old issues resumed in displaced or "coded" terms, a constant idea of the classical republican vision now excluded from the actual world. Nothing better illustrates this process of reverse imaging, perhaps, than Federalist feminism, the campaign for women's equality that is waged in *The Port Folio* on terms that always insist on mind or intellect as a wholly legitimate basis of social distinction. For the radical claim made by Federalist feminism during this period—that "women have been disgraced or degraded," as one *Port Folio* writer says, "in consequence of the neglect, indifference, or tyranny of man" (10:2:85)—originates in the equally radical claim that mind or intellect is the only basis of genuine civilization.

The oppression of women becomes in *The Port Folio* a virtual allegory of mind or intellect denied by mere philistinism, male prejudice as rooted in a brute strength that fears or is threatened by intelligence as such. "There are to be found men," says one female correspondent of *The American Lounger*, "so illiberal as to say, that, as women have no concern in the regulation of state affairs . . . it is ridiculous to bestow time and money in giving them a liberal education. Nay, there are some who go so far as to suppose our intellectual faculties are not sufficiently strong" (3:49). This is the world of male prejudice as it is gradually neutralized within the pages of *The Port Folio* by an increasingly confident Federalist feminism. "Wonderful as it may appear to you," says another female correspondent a few years later, "I do 'contend for an equality of genius between man and woman.' Our education is different, so are our modes of life. . . . Are not these causes sufficient to produce the difference between the sexes, without resorting to an original difference of mind?" (6:2:354).

The essence of Federalist feminism may be seen in the way such arguments simply pursue in other terms *The Port Folio*'s own earlier warfare against the rule of the demos, always pictured as the weight of a massive and complacent ignorance as it presses down on merit or virtue or intelligence. On a still partly comic or satiric level, this becomes for Federalist feminism the loutish husband who is made suspicious by any sign of intellectual seriousness in his wife. "For *The Port Folio* he has a great aversion," says one such woman, who has just been telling the story of how her husband constantly sabotages her study of French, "and protests that the wits of the half the women in town have been wool gathering ever since its publication" (5:113). On an altogether more serious level, it becomes the justifiable anger of women as they are excluded from real education in America by a conspiracy of male prejudice, power exercised by men to whom a woman is, as one writer puts it, nothing more than "a washing, baking, brewing, spinning, sewing, darning and child-producing animal" (10:2:85).[6]

Such opinions, repeated and elaborated during the latter years of Dennie's editorship, redraw in feminist terms the division or separation already assumed to exist between *The Port Folio* and the world: out there, where the demos now rules, is also a society in which men seriously doubt the existence of female intelligence, where women are denied access to real education,[7] and where women performing tasks identical to men are paid at a lower rate;[8] in here, within the pages of *The Port Folio* and the magic circumference of the republic of letters, women and men alike are valued in terms of what one feminist correspondent calls "their virtue, and their understanding." To the "self-important gentry" who deny female intellect, says this same writer, there is an obvious answer: tell them "to look through the republic of letters." For "the works of a More, a Carter, a Radcliffe, a D'Arblay, and a Dacier, will sail down the stream of time, notwithstanding all the opposing billows of envious illiberality" (3:49).

These are claims with a modern ring, and yet they are not modern claims, for at the heart of Federalist feminism lies the same vision of an aristocracy of mind or intellect that had in an earlier period motivated *The Port Folio*'s defense of classical education against "the equality of ignorance" insisted upon by Jeffersonian democracy.[9] Thus it is, for instance, that *The Port Folio* will associate itself with that tradition of Augustan feminism that satirizes female lightmindedness as a betrayal of women's intelligence—Pope's *To a Lady* or Belinda in *The Rape of the Lock* as these then lead to the portrayal of Miss Larolles in Burney's *Cecilia* or Lydia in Austen's *Pride and Prejudice*[10]—and thus it is that women writers whose work is vitiated by a shallow sentimentalism or second-hand sensationalism, the Hannah Fosters and Susanna Rowsons of the young republic, can be wryly dismissed by Oliver Oldschool as laboring for little more than "the emolument of the proprietor of a circulating library" (3:242).

The distinction between the circulating library and the private or public library stocked with works of genuine learning, by the same token, is the distinction between the two modes of reading that sustain, respectively, the public sphere of the demos and the republic of letters as now inhabited by literary Federalism. For the circulating library is for *The Port Folio* the very symbol of that eternal present of the demos in which reading persists as a mere cultural reflex, the world of *Charlotte Temple* and *The Coquette* and a thousand more forgotten titles,[11] where books are a disposable item, reading has become a mere leisure-time amusement, and it is possible to imagine, if one looks ahead in projected terms, an America in which, effectively speaking, no one reads anything at all. For *The Port Folio*, on the other hand, the true or serious library will remain right up to the end what it was at the beginning, what Dennie, discussing Davenant's *Gondibert*, once calls a "monument of banished souls" (3:171).

In the early years of *The Port Folio*, we have seen, the banished souls whose spirit lives on in libraries owe their existence to an ontology of reading that, while in one sense very old, is in another familiar to a reader in any age who has felt the world vanish while engrossed in a book. Thus *The Port Folio* will quote Dr. Aiken as saying that reading permits us to speak to Caesar or join the circle of Athenians listening to Socrates, the point being partly that we enter their world when we open the volume and turn the page, but partly too that our own world ceases to exist when we do so. This is in turn the phenomenon, at once so familiar and so strange, that implies the moral ontology always entailed by this idea of reading, the notion of a permanent and universal human nature that is everywhere the same. For the serious reader is always for literary Federalism, as an early essay in *The Port Folio* puts it, an "investigator of human nature": "No clime, no age, no nation will escape his penetrating eye" or "be incapable of furnishing some hints to a mind of intelligent observation" (2:283).

The reason that actual American society grows increasingly less real to *The Port Folio* in later years has to do with its recognition that the rule of the demos, which it has come only very gradually to understand as permanent and irreversible, is based on an opposing moral ontology, and in particular on the conviction that human nature in America is somehow importantly different than in other nations or ages. This is the deeper sense, as Joyce Appleby has pointed out, in which Federalism had been right all along to see Jeffersonian ideology as the triumph in America of French revolutionary thought, not at the level of doctrines about liberty and equality but at the far more fundamental level of a conception of human moral nature. "Moral light has darted its rays upon the world," proclaims one entirely representative Jeffersonian spokesman cited by Appleby. "It has . . . exalted the human character to a state of splendid greatness and perfectibility, that no former age has ever yet realized or experienced" (*Capitalism* 83).

Such claims seem to *The Port Folio* so transparently false or misleading that for a long while it is able to speak of Jeffersonian ideology only as an illusion, a dream, an evil enchantment laid upon the nation. This is the unreality that derives from the absurdity of imagining that human nature has changed in some radical way. For Dennie and the *Port Folio* writers, it will also always involve a proposition about literature, the impossibility of imagining a kind of reading in which one picked up Homer or Shakespeare and saw oneself as belonging to a different species than Odysseus or Hamlet or Falstaff—or, alternatively, a world in which such questions never arose because Homer and Shakespeare were not read at all. The unreality of Jeffersonian America does not lie for them simply in its antagonism towards liberal education or classical learning. This, after all, might be explained by a devotion to material gain at the expense of mind or intellect. The root of the matter is, rather, the Federalists' experience of their own way of reading as something so basic or primary that, until shown a society in which it has become alien or strange, they had imagined it as being simply the condition of literate consciousness.[12]

The paradox through which the republic of letters becomes more real to *The Port Folio* than the teeming actuality of the new American republic is thus in the end not paradoxical after all. For what has been at issue all along is the notion of human consciousness as a primary reality, the medium in which—though most of life consists of forgetting or ignoring the fact—the world has its only possible existence for us. For *The Port Folio* and its audience, this is preeminently a truth apprehended through language and books and reading, which is why literary Federalism in its last phase demands to be seen as a mode of literate consciousness struggling to sustain itself in an alien reality. The tendency most powerfully at work in *The Port Folio* during this period will be toward a reconstitution of the world in moral and imaginative terms, as though history and society, no longer representing a reality with which one might engage directly through political action, may only be rematerialized as objects of purely literary contemplation.

This new sense of imaginative detachment pervades Francis Kinloch's *Letters from Geneva*, a remarkable account, serialized in *The Port Folio* over a period of seventeen months, of an American Federalist traveling through a Europe still trying to recover from the cataclysmic upheaval of the French revolutionary wars. "The gentry of Savoy," observes Kinloch at one point, "have suffered almost as much as the clergy. They have . . . been ruined by fines and confiscations, while a new race of people . . . has risen to opulence and to distinction, in their place. At Salenches, I was looking at the castle, and asked a person who came up, the name of the proprietor. It has been confiscated, he said, and sold for assignats, and now belongs to the barber, who used formerly to shave Monsieur le Baron." And then, without a break, without even the indentation of a paragraph that would signal a shift of mood or matter, Kinloch goes on: "The moonlight view of Chamourny is extremely sublime" (8:2:131).

At such moments we glimpse the process through which the French Revolution is being transformed for literary Federalism into history, and at the same time the process through which, precisely because the world after the French Revolution resembles nothing that has ever gone before, history has ceased to exist as a source of civic wisdom and is on its way to becoming something else, an imaginative refuge for those souls to whom the modern age seems a shrunken or degraded reality. This is the principle on which the ancient world, which for *The Port Folio* just a few years before had been a living moral ideal, is most often represented in the *Letters from Geneva* as ruins: "Nimes was once, under the government of the Romans, a city of great extent, but of its ancient walls nothing now remains, but one solitary dismantled tower, which is at a considerable distance from the modern town; it contains, however, more Roman antiquities and in a greater state of preservation than any town in France" (8:1:273).

The majesty of these ruins, by the same token, permits us to see that they have begun to appear to the Federalist mind as a memorial not simply of Roman civilization but of the classical republican vision that had once hoped for the return of greatness in the modern age, and that had been able briefly to glimpse in the America of Washington and Hamilton an actual rebirth of the Roman republic of Cincinnatus and Scipio. Now all this, as in Kinloch's description of a Roman amphitheater, has returned to stone: "We remained for some time in silent contemplation of this mighty edifice. It seemed worthy of those who had been masters of the world, and they now appeared to us capable of having performed all the great things which history has attributed to them. Upwards of seventeen hundred years had rolled away since the amphitheater was built, and yet where avarice or the fury of an enemy have not made great efforts to destroy it, the parts are as entire as if it had been erected in the last century" (8:1:274).

Such moments mark *The Port Folio*'s discovery of mind or consciousness as a last unsuspected source of republican virtue in an otherwise fallen social reality. For the sense of melancholy or cultural mourning evident here and elsewhere in the *Letters from Geneva* is something superposed on the ruins by the mind of the observer,[13] and its meaning as a meditation on vanished greatness has to do with moral grandeur rather than with arches and carved stones. To see this is suddenly and unexpectedly to have seen as well that the glory of Periclean Greece or the early Roman republic had originated not in populousness or power or wealth but in a moral state attainable by human consciousness. The notion that *virtus* may then survive in certain minds when the republic has been lost had in eighteenth-century England become an axiom of literary Augustanism, always invoked to explain how a Virgil or a Livy could have emerged when Rome was under the rule of an emperor. "Though the republic was subverted," Gibbon will declare in a "Life of Virgil" republished in *The Port Folio*, "the minds of the Romans remained republican" (7:1:168).

The process through which *The Port Folio* comes to an identical conclusion about its own relation to Jeffersonian democracy marks, in an important sense, the formal genesis of literary Federalism. For this is when certain Federalist writers would come to see, as writers in the ancient world had seen long before, that to minds still republican in spirit there remains an unexpected resource, literary style as the revelation in language of a consciousness for which *virtus* has not ceased to be real. The great example is Cicero, retiring amidst the ruins of the republic to Tusculum, there to write the works of philosophy and political theory that would serve the Renaissance humanists as their supreme model of literary style. But then, in the tradition that becomes exemplary for literary Federalism in the moment of its vanishing, come such later Latin authors as Tacitus and Pliny and, in English, those Augustan writers for whom the very basis of literary expression had been the steady moral consciousness of an older, nobler time.

For Dennie and *The Port Folio* this is, as always, the line that culminates in Goldsmith, through the magic of whose style a vision of organic society has been permitted to survive in language as a last refuge from the degradations of Jeffersonian America. "The very bane of style," says Dennie, introducing a memoir of Goldsmith in words that might be taken as the last testament of literary Federalism, "is the habit of reading the vulgar vehicles of democratic folly," the "ephemeral imbecility" that one comes upon in "so many of our This, That, and 'Tother Gazettes." The symbol of *virtus* in a fallen social reality becomes in this context—it is the very moment when literary Federalism vanishes as a mode of civic consciousness to reappear as a style or mode of writing—becomes the "high-spirited young man" whom Dennie urges to "avert his eyes from false models, and gaze steadfastly upon the true. Let Sir William Temple, Dean Swift, Lord Bolingbroke,

Dryden, Addison, Johnson, Burke and Goldsmith be his constant companions" (8:2:261).

This is the moment, too, at which a reader of *The Port Folio* begins to realize that the transmutation of republican virtue into literary style, though unannounced as such, has in fact been taking place all along, and that the symbol of its completion is going to be the transfer of Goldsmith's mantle, as the last great Augustan stylist, to the young Washington Irving in America. For Irving, who from the beginning has taken Goldsmith as his own literary model, has also specifically been writing under the sign of literary Federalism, as a disciple of Oliver Oldschool. The Irving who finds himself being chided good-humoredly by Dennie in 1803—under the name "Jonathan Oldstyle" he has been writing for *The Morning Chronicle* of New York, known, observes Dennie, for its "jacobinical tendencies"—is already visible as an heir apparent: "We hope that the appellation of 'Oldstyle' is not a misnomer. The Oldstyles, agreeably to ancient heraldry, have always been considered a branch of the Oldschool" (3:13).

Even at so early a juncture, one is able to glimpse the source of Irving's immediate authority within literary Federalism in an idealizing vision of traditional society that, though in some obvious sense deriving from such works as Goldsmith's *The Vicar of Wakefield*, may now be represented as belonging neither to England nor America but to the republic of letters. By the time Dennie's editorship of *The Port Folio* ends nearly a decade later, Irving and the *Salmagundi* group will have emerged as the legitimate successors, appearing belatedly and unexpectedly in distant America, of the literary congeries of eighteenth-century London, the Scriblerus Club of Pope and Swift or the brilliant Club dominated by Johnson's majestic personality a generation later. This will be the theme of *The Stranger in New York*, a series of letters in *The Port Folio* purportedly written by an Englishman aiming to set straight the false impression given by travelers who have seen nothing in America but a philistine worship of wealth. Thus the poet Moore has reported, says the Stranger, that the people, from "the influence of republican sentiments, are strangers to taste, refinement, and the arts of imagination: are vulgar, unsocial, insolent, and avaricious," and thus the German traveler Bulow, given to a certain Prussian bluntness, has found them "a mean, grovelling, avaricious, and barbarous herd" (11:2:586).

To such verdicts as this *The Stranger in New York* ostensibly objects, adducing the very existence of the *Salmagundi* group as evidence that "vigor and brilliancy" of literary imagination can flourish even under American conditions. Yet really *The Stranger* is meant as an indirect confirmation of such travelers as Bulow and Moore—both of whom, after all, had been given prominent voice in *The Port Folio* during its period of direct engagement with Jeffersonian democracy—and it becomes clear that Irving and his fellows, to whom now has been passed the torch of literary Federalism, are being celebrated for having created in language a separate world. Thus it is that the Stranger, when he comes to sketch his portrait of Irving, will draw on just the vocabulary Dennie has always used in speaking of Goldsmith, praising him for "a taste delicate and refined" and "a humor rich and playful," and, even more significantly, will borrow to express his own summary judgment on Irving's writings Dr. Johnson's observations on the genius of Addison.[14]

The Irving praised in such terms is the writer whose redemptive vision of a lost traditional society is already evident in his Jonathan Old-style letters and *History of New York*—what the Stranger calls his "Knickerbocker"—and who in a few short years will embark on the long European exile that demands to be seen, in relation to later American literary tradition, as itself a symbolic episode.[15] For the movement towards literature as a separate reality or world elsewhere that is visible in *The Port Folio* during the last years of Dennie's editorship will culminate not simply in works like *Bracebridge Hall*, nor in a certain moral perspective that then persists in Melville, Thoreau, and Hawthorne, but in the Saturday Club and a constellation of writers— Holmes, Motley, Lowell, Longfellow, Charles Eliot Norton—whose works would subsequently be eclipsed by a more acceptably "democratic" literary canon. This is the sense, as I began by suggesting in the preface, that one does not hear the last dying echoes of literary Federalism until the very end of the century, in the work of such writers as Henry Adams and Henry James and Santayana.

In February 1812, readers of *The Port Folio* opened the magazine to learn that Joseph Dennie was no more. Along with the advancement of literature, says the author of an extended mortuary notice summarizing Dennie's life and career, his great object had been to reclaim "the youth of America from the low career of sordid interests." This is Dennie as he saw himself, as an embattled spirit in a nation antagonistic to mind or intellect, a hero of literature—of the very possibility of literature—in an America that has no use for books or reading. At first, says the memorialist, he stood almost alone, but then, the example of his indomitability having "a magical power," genuinely gifted men and women had rallied to his standard: "such is the power of a single mind in awakening the talents of a whole nation," that "the establishment of his work may be considered as forming an era in the literary history of

America" (12:1:186). Even in the ceremonious solemnity of this memo-rialist's utterance we may hear, if we listen, the troubled echoes of an earlier combat, those days of open engagement when *The Port Folio* had counterposed to Jeffersonian democracy a classical republican vision of the new American polity, and then, that battle lost, had struggled to es-tablish literature as a sphere of imaginative reality isolated from the degradation of life in a nation taking as its gospel Jeffersonian democ-racy and *The Way to Wealth*.

The *Port Folio* that announces Dennie's death contains, at the end of the memorial pages on him, a funeral engraving: a tomb surmounted by an urn, a classically draped female figure, the Muse of poetry or imaginative writing, bent weeping over the grave. There is a radiant laurel crown suspended in the sky just above the sad tableau, meant to suggest, in the symbolism of an ancient iconography, the imperishabil-ity of Dennie's reputation as an author and editor of genius. On the urn, just visible beneath the drape of a funeral shroud, one sees the first few letters of Dennie's name. On the pictured tombstone, just below, is a motto taken with one minor verbal variation from a longer epitaph that Dennie when alive would have known by heart: *nihil quod tetigit non ornavit*. It is the motto Dennie might have chosen for himself, in a brave hope that there might never cease to exist an America in which there would survive some few souls able to read the words and, read-ing them, to call to mind the world in which they had once been composed.

Notes

Chapter One: The Demon Democracy

1. *The Port Folio*, volume 1, page 4. Since the original volume and page numbering of the magazine is inordinately complicated—Dennie began numbering over again from volume 1 in January 1806 when *The Port Folio* inaugurated its new series, and on that occasion he also abandoned the folio format for octavo—I have for ease of reference adopted a simplified system of citation. Between 1801 and 1805, parenthetical references are simply to volume and page. Thus, for instance, the above reference would be given in the text as follows: (1:4). After 1806, parenthetical references are as follows: (year:volume number:page). Thus a reference to a passage appearing in *The Port Folio* for 24 September 1808 would appear as follows: (8:2:214).

2. For general background, see Pocock, *The Machiavellian Moment*. For the specific relation between Federalism and classical republican thought, see Dowling, *Poetry and Ideology in Revolutionary Connecticut*.

3. Appleby gives in *Capitalism and a New Social Order* an exemplary account of Federalism as a variant of classical republican thought, as well as the way the French Revolution served to catalyze opposition between Federalists and Jeffersonians:

> The opposing views finally stood opposed. To the Federalists the French Revolution was the source of the delusions and enthusiasms that could undermine civil order as it had been understood for generations in America. . . . Federalists, however, were not mindless conservatives. Having participated in the American Revolution they warmly affirmed the freedom of self-governing, autonomous men and accepted the ex-

tended suffrage of American states. Federalists' values embraced the mobility of the meritorious—what they considered the just reward for diligence in a lawful calling—but in all essentials they remained classical republicans. Their political faith represented a modification, not a rejection, of traditional expectations about the role of authority in public life, about the permanence of social classes and the desirable distance between the governed and the governors. (59)

Appleby also gives a fine summary account of the ideal of "positive liberty" lying at the heart of Federalist thought:

> To have liberty was to share in the power of the state, to be actively involved in making and executing decisions. Thus liberty in this sense was associated with a republic—the rule of law—and could not exist in a monarchy where the will of the king or queen was supreme. Liberty in the classical republican tradition pertained to the public realm and not the private. Indeed, it was the capacity of men to rise above personal interest that made republics and therefore liberty possible. Virtue and liberty were indissolubly linked in classical republican theory. (16)

More recently, James Roger Sharp has argued at length in *American Politics in the Early Republic* that the ideological divisions of the 1790s in effect turned on the question of which group had the truer understanding of the classical republican inheritance. "The new frame of government, as ratified in 1788, was influenced by the overly optimistic, classical republican, civic humanist assumption the selfless representatives of the citizenry could and would come together and legislate for the national public good and that this public good somehow could and would be determinable" (2). As a consequence, "Americans of differing political persuasions could with great sincerity and conviction argue that they, and they *alone*, reflected the national public good" (3).

4. The allegiance of the Jeffersonians to Country party terminology was strong enough to lead them to try to brand Hamilton a "new Walpole" in the early years of the Washington administration (see McCoy 136–65). Yet this was an attempt that never rose above the transient level of party rhetoric, one remembered now mainly by historians of banking and the funding system.

5. Dennie and the *Port Folio* writers during the first term of Jefferson's presidency tended to view themselves as "Augustan" in the sense that I have examined at length in *Poetry and Ideology in Revolutionary Connecticut*, taking over from the English Augustan poets an idea of poetry as a mode of symbolic action able to alter the course of history:

> The long warfare of Pope and Swift and Thomson and a hundred lesser poets of the literary Opposition against Walpole was not simply a visible symptom of some underlying crisis having to do with violently altering

property relations and ideological breakdown: the poets were at the very center of that crisis, battling through their chosen means of language and myth to bring it to a conclusion favorable to the moral regeneration of English society, and the general breakdown of ideology is a measure of their power over events. So far as their relentless unmasking of Walpole and the Robinocracy then cleared the space for the later success of Country ideology in the American colonies, poets like Pope and Thomson must be viewed as moving spirits of the Revolution. (xiv–xv)

The Federalist writers in the earliest stages of their warfare against Jeffersonian "democratic republicanism" undertook their unmasking of Jefferson and the Virginia oligarchy on precisely similar grounds.

6. See Hazen 173–86. Referring to the excitement which prevailed in Philadelphia in 1793–94, John Adams, in a letter to Thomas Jefferson written many years afterward, said: 'You certainly never felt the terrorism excited by Genet in 1793 when ten thousand people in the streets of Philadelphia day after day threatened to drag Washington out of his house and effect a revolution in the government or compel it to declare war in favor of the French Revolution and against England'" (Hazen 186).

7. In 1801, Dennie lists the Federalist papers as follows: "the Centinel, Washington Federalist, Gazette of the United States, . . . the Trenton Federalist . . . the Connecticut Courant, the Walpole Museum, the Hampshire Gazette, the Worcester paper, and many others" (1:286).

8. A sense of the French Revolution as a universal ideological movement is strong in *The Port Folio* from the very beginning. Thus, for instance, a reviewer of Gentz's "On the origin and character of the war against the French Revolution" quotes from his records of debates in the Jacobin club in 1791:

Thus, on the 15th of December, 1791, Brissot, in a speech to the club, says, he has from the beginning of the revolution been convinced, that a people conquering their liberty require war. . . . "The shock we shall communicate in every country, where we carry our arms, will rapidly spread; we shall electrify every heart; we shall sound the alarum-bell, at which all nations awake. Providence seems to have decreed, that the earth should from time to time be subject to certain great revolutions. Think of the crusades. The crusade of universal freedom is opening. Every soldier will be a Peter, a Bernard, but with infinitely more eloquence. He will preach, not mystical doctrines, but what every one knows and wishes—the end of slavery." (1:302)

9. The attitude the *Port Folio* writers saw as incomprehensible is that summed up in Jefferson's famous "Adam and Eve" letter, the significance of which, in the wake of Joseph Ellis's *American Sphinx* and Conor Cruise O'Brien's *The Long Affair*, has once again begun to be seriously debated. James Roger Sharp gives a balanced account of the letter:

In a rather remarkable letter, Jefferson reproved his old friend and protégé, William Short, for criticizing the course of the French Revolution.
Jefferson had a tendency to engage in hyperbole and, at the time he
wrote the letter, he was not fully aware of the violent turn the revolution
had taken, but Jefferson's letter to Short is spontaneous and immediate
and captures the almost euphoric hopes and excitement Jefferson felt at
the prospects of the revolution and the fears he had about the subversion
of republicanism in America. "The liberty of the whole earth," Jefferson
wrote Short, depended on the success of the French Revolution, "and
was ever such a prize won with so little innocent blood?" Although Jefferson reported that he had lost some close friends in the terror, he said
that rather than see the revolution fail, he "would have seen half the
earth desolated." Were "there but an Adam and Eve left in every country, and left free, it would be better than as it now is." (73)

Joseph Ellis's comment is pertinent to an understanding of the Federalists' response to Jefferson's Jacobin sympathies: "Such an extreme version of what
might be called revolutionary realism, which conjures up comparisons to the
twentieth-century radicals in the Lenin or Mao mold, exposes a chilling side of
Jefferson's character that seems so thoroughly incongruous with his temperament and so resolutely ideological. But his casual response to the atrocities of
the French Revolution was in fact an integral part of a rather deeply felt sense
of where history was headed" (127).

10. The quote from Moore is taken from Kerber's *Federalists in Dissent*
(51–52), which gives a useful bibliography of the historiography of the Hemings episode and lists all numbers of *The Port Folio* in which it is mentioned. In
her coauthored article on the Adams family's contributions to *The Port Folio*,
Kerber observes that J. Q. Adams's adaptations of Horace's Xanthia ode proves
that "Adams was not above putting his literary talents to low service" (457). As
will be clear from my own discussion, I think Adams himself would have
viewed the ode in rather a different light.

11. Federalists were convinced that the three-fifths rule had provided Jefferson's margin of victory in the 1800 election. Thus, for instance, Fisher Ames:
"let none but the stupidest of the rabble be deceived by their hypocrisy, when
they dare to say, the will of the people ought to prevail. They know that without the black votes, Mr. Jefferson would not have been president; they know
that these black votes are given in contempt of the rights of man; for the Virginia negroes have no more political will or power than the cattle on the Ken-
nebec" (*Works* 266).

In The Road to Division: Secessionists at Bay, 1776–1884, William W. Freehling
undertakes an exhaustive statistical analysis that reaches the same conclusion.
On Freehling's analysis, Adams would have won the election 63–61, the South
losing fourteen electoral votes owed to the three-fifths rule.

12. Taken from McCoy (12), whose informative treatment of the intellectual
background my own discussion assumes.

13. See my *Poetry and Ideology in Revolutionary Connecticut*, chapter 3. Particularly relevant to the georgic in its American context are Rosenmeyer, Miles, and Rōstvig.

14. Exploitation of Native Americans for purposes of land speculation is a recurrent theme in *The Port Folio*. Thus, for instance, a reviewer of James Sullivan's *History of the District of Maine* points out that the Indians who have been inveigled into "selling" their land have no concept of private property in the European sense, so that even the concept of land sale depends on a fetishization of property invisible to those whose thought has been shaped by Lockean contract theory:

> "The purchases were always of a sachem, or of some one who pretended to that dignity of character. And that if the Indians made a chief, for the purpose of leading them in war, and to declare when a war should begin, and when it would by no means follow that he should have power to sell their lands. The Indian conveyances clearly amounted to nothing more, than a contract, made by the chief, on consent of his tribe, that the savages should not make war on the white people, for taking lands to a certain extent into possession. In this way, we may account for one sachem's selling the same tract to several different purchasers; for, if the deed was only an agreement upon peace and friendship, there could, in the Indian's view, be no immorality in making the contract with as many as might appear to demand it. And a wish in some of the savages to trade with the white people, and to learn the art of agriculture, might be a principle motive." This mode of deducing a title is somewhat singular. (1:331)

Similarly, a reviewer of Jonathan Boucher's *A View of the Causes and Consequences of the American Revolution* energetically dissents from Boucher's notion that white settlement has been a "civilizing" influence on Native Americans: "The project of christianizing the Indians, seems destined to be abortive, unless we can contrive to live somewhat more like christians than we do at present. For, as long as they see citizens only in the light of robbers of land, and sellers of rum and whiskey, it is vain to hope, that they can be induced to think favorably of our religion" (1:218).

15. This was not exclusively a New England view. James Roger Sharp quotes John Taylor of Caroline to the effect that Connecticut had long enjoyed a genuinely democratic form of government: "He vehemently denied what he thought Jefferson seemed to be implying—that 'persons, sufficiently malignant to destroy the public good,' were 'naturally the issue of every popular government.' For proof he cited the experience of 'Connecticut, which has [for] about two centuries enjoyed a compleat unanimity under a government, the most democratic of any representative form which every existed'" (191). For a Connecticut Federalist like Timothy Dwight, the point missed by Taylor would be that Connecticut's long history of participatory democracy had been founded on a collective moral character made possible only by the classical republican ideal of positive liberty: in the South, where Federalists saw moral character as

having been irreparably vitiated by slaveholding and doctrines of radical individualism, Dwight—and, on the evidence, Joseph Dennie and most of his contributors—would have denied that such participatory democracy was possible.

16. The best historical treatment of the early republic viewed in this light is to be found in the work of those whom Winifred Barr Rothenberg has called the "moral economy" historians: see in particular Henretta and Kulikoff. So far as Rothenberg is herself strongly critical of the "moral economy" school, the disagreement is one among social and economic historians. The interest of their work for students of early republican literature seems to me to lie in the way they have tried to recover the underlying assumptions about human nature and society evident in works like Dennie's *Lay Preacher* essays and Dwight's *Travels*.

17. The reason that Jeffersonian agrarianism was so specifically able to neutralize Federalist criticism, I think, lies in the centrality to Federalist thinking of the classical republican theory of cyclical history. Drew McCoy has argued that Jefferson's idea of land as an illimitable source of civic virtue implies an escape from historical cyclicality; this is the deeper significance of the Jeffersonian "vision of a predominantly agricultural empire that would expand across space, rather than develop through time" (McCoy 186).

Chapter Two: Oliver Oldschool

1. The author is never identified. Dennie says only, in one of his later columns addressed "To Readers and Correspondents," that the essay "originally appeared in the Fredericktown Herald, a paper, which we read often, and highly commend" (4:247).

2. This is "traffic" in its normal eighteenth-century sense of trade or commerce (OED def. 2: "The buying or selling or exchange of goods for profit"), but also, one suspects, with a hint of its more negative modern connotation (see OED def. 6).

3. "This metaphysics of community is underwritten at a deeper level, however, by a metaphysics of being and nonbeing or life and death already archaic at the time Aristotle was writing the *Politics*, a submerged collective memory of the warrior ethos in which the survival of the polity as a whole, its art and its thought and its ordinary life of field and village, is reducible in an absolutely literal sense to the willingness of a relatively small number of males to die on behalf of those too young or old or weak to go forth in battle" (*Hellenism and Homosexuality* 7).

Charles Taylor gives a good short summary of the "Machiavellian" formulation in *Philosophical Arguments*:

We could say that a free, that is, participatory regime calls on citizens to provide for themselves things that a despotism may provide for them. The foremost example of this is national defense. A despotic regime may raise money and hire mercenaries to fight for it; a republican regime will generally call on its citizens to fight for their own freedom. The causal links run in both directions. Citizen armies guarantee freedom because they are an obstacle to despotic takeover, just as large armies at the disposal of powerful generals invite a coup, as the agony of the Roman republic demonstrates. But at the same time, only people who live in and cherish a free regime will be motivated to fight for themselves. This relation between citizen armies and freedom was one of the main themes of Machiavelli's work. (193)

4. The degree to which this view was a matter of deep personal conviction is caught in a letter written by Fisher Ames to George Richard Minot on 3 May 1789, describing Washington's address to the combined houses of the new Congress:

> I still think of him with more veneration than for any other person. Time has made havoc upon his face. That, and many other circumstances not to be reasoned about, conspire to keep up the awe which I brought with me. He addressed the two Houses in the Senate chamber; it was a very touching scene, and quite of the solemn kind. His aspect grave, almost to sadness; his modesty, actually shaking; his voice deep, a little tremulous, and so low as to call for close attention; added to the series of objects presented to the mind, and overwhelming it, produced emotions of the most affecting kind upon the members. I, Pilgaric, sat entranced. It seemed to me an allegory in which virtue was personified, and addressing those whom she would make her votaries. Her power over the heart was never greater, and the illustration of her doctrine by her own example was never more perfect. (568)

5. *Works*, 203. The passage from which this is taken nicely demonstrates Ames's sense of what might be called the Leninist dimension of the ideology of progress:

> They at last make conscience of committing the most shocking atrocities, and learn to throw their eyes beyond the gulf of revolution, confusion, and civil war, which yawns at their feet, to behold an Eden of primitive innocence, equality, and liberty in blossom on the other side. There these tigers of revolution, their leaders, are to lie down with the lamb-like multitude, sometimes suffering hunger yet forbearing to eat them. The rights of man are to be established by being solemnly proclaimed, and printed, so that every citizen shall have a copy. Avarice, ambition, revenge, and rage will be disenchanted from all hearts and die there; man will be regenerated; by slaying half a million only once, four millions will be born twice, and the glorious work of that perfectibility of the species, foretold by Condorcet and the Mazzei sect in America, will begin.

6. Robert Ferguson makes what I take to be a similar point in his account of the "pessimism" of Federalist lawyers during the period of the Jeffersonian ascendancy:

One after the other, the leading intellectuals of the early bar gave way to the gloomiest predictions. Progressive historians have tended to dismiss this pessimism as narrow-mindedness, but it was the presence of vision, not its absence, that brought despair to the likes of Fisher Ames, Gouverneur Morris, William Wirt, John Quincy Adams, and Daniel Webster. Well versed in classical models of government, the early American lawyer rarely forgot that his favorite heroes from antiquity, the lawyer-orators Demosthenes and Cicero, died resisting the successful efforts of despots to subvert republican rule. His readings in Thucydides, Plutarch, Tacitus, Machiavelli, and Montesquieu left him brooding over, in Joseph Story's words, "the melancholy lessons of the past history of republics down to our own." (206)

7. Ferguson recounts a wonderful anecdote that serves to demonstrate how strongly the Federalist view of classical education would insensibly influence the attitudes even of those in the opposing party:

An incident involving James Kent, later the chancellor of New York, and Edward Livingston, who would codify Louisiana law and become secretary of state under Andrew Jackson, illustrates the power of that affinity. Riding circuit together as young lawyers in 1786, Kent noted in his journal that Livingston "had a pocket Horace and read some passages to me, and pointed out their beauties, assuming that I well understood Horace. I said nothing, but was stung with shame and mortification. I purchased immediately Horace and Virgil . . . and formed my resolution, promptly and decidedly, to recover the lost languages." Soon Kent was devoting early mornings to Latin and Greek, late afternoons to French, and evenings to English literature in a prodigious quest for "solid happiness and honor." (27)

Chapter Three: The Philosophy of Merriment

1. Thus Thomas Mayo in *Epicurus in England:* "The independent cities had been swallowed in the unwieldy post-Alexandrian empire of the eastern Mediterranean. His part of the world was ruled by hybrid emperors never seen by most of their millions of subjects. Great strange armies swept periodically across the land in confused and meaningless struggles. . . . The ordinary citizen, repelled by a public life grown too vast and complex for him to grasp, was thus driven to work out some philosophy that would give significance to his own tiny separate existence" (xviii–xix). See also Farrington, *The Faith of Epicurus.*

2. Cf. Moore's remarks on the College of William and Mary, which he surely knew to be Jefferson's alma mater, and which he doubtless knew from Dennie and his friends to have abolished Greek and Latin as entrance requirements at Jefferson's urging: "The college of William and Mary, the only one in the state of Virginia, and the first which I saw in America, gave me but a

96

melancholy idea of republican seats of learning. That contempt for the elegan-
cies of education which the American democrats affect, is nowhere more
grossly conspicuous than in Virginia. . . . As every thing that distinguishes
from the multitude is supposed to be invidious and unpopular, the leveling
system is applied to education, and has all the effect its partisans could desire,
by producing a most extensive equality of ignorance" (6:2:88–89).

   3. Robert Ferguson's treatment of Irving's career tends to interpret in personal terms what I am here describing as the Federalist retreat from history.
For instance: "As early as 1823, Irving summarized the new patterns that
would dominate all of his later writings: 'I prefer summon[ing] up the bright
pictures of life that I have witnessed and dwelling as much as possible on the
agreeable.' Creativity meant 'an activity in my imagination . . . apt to soften
and tint up the harshest realities.' The satirist has withdrawn" (170).

   As will be evident from my discussion so far, such sentiments on Irving's
part seem to me to be intelligible only when read against the background of the
"philosophy of merriment" as discussed in this chapter. Indeed, my sense is
that only a sympathetic understanding of literary Federalism provides the
grounds on which it is possible to make genuine sense of Irving's writings and
career as a whole.

Chapter Four: The Republic of Letters

   1. The title of the essay is "Universal Peace in the Realms of Literature."
The peace thus celebrated is within the ranks of Federalism: John Quincy
Adams's recently published *Lectures on Eloquence* had been given a favorable
review in *The Monthly Anthology*, at this point the very voice of Boston Federalism. This the Beehive writer takes to signal an amnesty between the Adams
and Hamilton wings of the Federal party, especially souls embittered by what
they considered to be John Quincy Adams's earlier desertion to the Jeffersonian side. For the *Monthly Anthology* reviewer, though making it clear that he
continues to disagree with Adams in politics, had made equally clear his conviction that literature, the subject of Adams's *Lectures*, should be taken to represent a separate realm of reality, a refuge (as he puts it) from the "tumults and
contentions" of public life, "a spot where we may escape . . . and enjoy that repose which we find nowhere else." This is why the *Beehive* writer so greatly re-
joices now in the Adams review: in a country "where party passions too
frequently reign uncontrolled," all reasonable souls must welcome "any effort
to circumscribe their sway—to screen from it the retreats of literature as a sanctum sanctorum."

   2. 5:295. The passage comes from a British essayist whose opinions Dennie
uses, in typical fashion, to comment obliquely on changes in *The Port Folio*'s
sense of its own ideological situation. For another passage from the same essay,
quoted in connection with *The Port Folio*'s dawning awareness of "the death of
the polis" as a workable moral and political ideal, see chapter 2, pp. 44–45.

3. The passage is taken from a prospectus issued by Wright, Goodenow, and Stockwell to announce an "improved" *Gazette*. The quoted passage is a translation from the French of "the venerable St. Pierre" (5:375).

4. (1:11). The occasion is *The Port Folio's* publication of letters from Boswell to an American correspondent. The importance of Johnson as a symbolic figure for literary Federalism may be inferred from Dennie's prefatory comment that "every thing, pertinent to the history of the illustrious Dr. Johnson, is highly interesting to the learned and to the moral" (1:10). The tendency of Federalist writers to perceive Johnson as an embattled hero of orthodoxy in an age of doubt and skepticism derives, no doubt, from the way Boswell's *Life of Johnson* was read, in both England and America, in the period immediately following the French Revolution. For more on this theme, see Dowling, *The Boswellian Hero*.

5. The issue arises most poignantly in connection with a correspondent's charge that Dennie, because he has questioned the stylistic purity of certain American linguistic usages, has given "proof of antipathy to America" (63). Dennie's reply is superb and, for an understanding of literary Federalism, crucial. First, he asks, sensibly enough, "what connection subsists between a philological discussion and the love of one's country?" Then he goes on at eloquent length about his own relation to America, concluding thus: "the Editor is an American: he educated himself in America; he lives in America; and as he does not contemplate a change in his situation, the probability is that he will die in America. He has some stake in the country" (7:1:63).

6. There is a conscious echo here, I think, of Burke's famous passage in *Reflections on the Revolution* in France on the doctrines of abstract equality that he saw as underlying the humiliation and ultimately the judicial murder of the king and queen by the revolutionaries:

All the decent drapery of life is to be rudely torn off. All the superadded ideas, furnished from the wardrobe of a moral imagination, which the heart owns, and the understanding ratifies, as necessary to cover the defects of our naked shivering nature, and to raise it to dignity in our own estimation, are to be exploded as a ridiculous, absurd, and antiquated fashion. On this scheme of things, a king is but a man; a queen is but a woman; a woman is but an animal, and an animal not of the highest order. (67)

7. The Federalist emphasis on a relation between intellect and virtue serves to explain, for instance, why Timothy Dwight, called the "Pope of Federalism" by his Jeffersonian detractors in Connecticut, had earlier been a pioneer of female education in his academy at Greenfield Hill. See Howard, *The Connecticut Wits*, 206–8.

8. The issue arises specifically in a feature serialized in *The Port Folio* as "The Table D'Hote": "The low rate of female labor is a grievance of the very first magnitude, and pregnant with the most mighty ills to society. . . . This unjust arrangement of remuneration for services performed diminishes the im-

portance of women in society—renders them more helpless and dependent. . . . It is difficult to conceive why, even in those branches wherein both sexes are engaged, there should be such an extreme of disparity in the recompense of labor as every person acquainted with the subject knows to exist" (10:1:319–20).

9. The phrase occurs in Thomas Moore's description of William and Mary College. See above, chapter 3, note 2.

10. Thus, for instance, the letter in an early *Port Folio* (1:101) from "Emilia" complaining that the magazine contains nothing for women ("What now, do you think we care for your remarks on Shakespeare . . . your philosophical Farrago?"). This is Federalist feminism in its satiric register: "Really, Mr. Oldschool, you pay us very little attention—and we are exceedingly displeased. Where are those 'gallant Mercutios and Rangers,' whom you invited so prettily to entertain us, more than a month ago? . . . It is true, I did hear a gentleman exclaim, and with some indignation too, that the women who read your paper, wanted not such trash; but we thought him a fool, and laughed at him accordingly."

11. For an exhaustive treatment of this body of writing, see Davidson's *Revolution and the Word*.

12. Thus, for instance, Charles Nisbet, president of Dickinson College and a close friend of Dennie, may be heard in *The Port Folio* to make the serious claim that jacobinism cannot survive a classical education: "A modern infidel, whether of the school of Voltaire, Rousseau or Hume, is as incapable of subscribing the creed of the classics, as of equalling their genius and abilities. The classics are too faithful to nature, and too near the simple and incorrupt state of mankind, to favor those degrading notions of our nature which modern infidels have prostituted their powers to support, for the service of Vice and Materialism" (8:1:76).

13. The extraordinary fact is that, although the writer of the *Letters* and his company never go to Rome, he indulges in a long meditation on the land of sloth and servitude that is modern Italy. The tone is pure Addison and Dyer, a demonstration that the *Letters* as they appear in *The Port Folio* are meant as a history lesson for American readers. The writer closes with a description from Chateaubriand:

A growth of withered grass, which the eye of the traveller easily mistakes for the promises of a plentiful harvest, very frequently conceals the traces of some ancient road: . . . no laborers are seen at work, no flocks and herds are wandering at large, hardly a tree gives variety to the scene, which is made up of ruined aqueducts and tombs, with here and there a miserable house either deserted altogether, or guarded by some poor wretch, a prey to poverty and fever. . . . It is in the midst of this sad scene, this extent of dreary and inhospitable wilds, that the immortal city presents itself, a city which has twice and for a lapse of ages governed mankind, which has survived so many vicissitudes, and which now in its decline gives rise to recollections that elevate the mind of the beholder, and warm his heart to pity. (8:215–16)

14. "The following observations, which Dr. Johnson applies to our countryman Addison, are extremely apposite to the present remarks. 'It appears from his various pictures of life, that he had conversed with many distinct classes of men, and marked with great acuteness the effects of different modes of life. He was a man in whose presence nothing reprehensible was out of danger, quick in discerning what was wrong or ridiculous, nor unwilling to expose it. Though his pleasure was rather to detect follies, than crimes, more to excite merriment than detestation'" (12:1:32–33).

15. It is treated as such by Jeffrey Rubin-Dorsky in *Washington Irving Adrift in the Old World*, though with conclusions rather different than those being drawn here.

A Note on Sources

THE pioneering work on Dennie was Ellis's *Joseph Dennie and His Circle* (1915); despite some minor inaccuracies, it remains a valuable guide to, especially, the period of the original *Lay Preacher* essays and *The Farmer's Museum*. To the period of Dennie's editorship of *The Port Folio*, the single best introduction is Joseph T. Queenan's University of Pennsylvania dissertation, "*The Port Folio*: A Study of the History and Significance of an American Magazine" (1955). A particular virtue of Queenan's study, which was unfortunately never published as a book, is the systematic and resourceful use it makes of various related primary materials, in particular those in the Biddle family papers in the Library of Congress and the Biddle, Cadwallader, and Meredith collections at the Pennsylvania Historical Society.

Contributions to *The Port Folio* were, according to the conventions governing periodical writing at the time, for the most part either anonymous or pseudonymous. On the grounds that this constitutes an important dimension of their contemporary meaning, I have with a few exceptions treated them as such in my discussion. The authorship of most contributions during the period of Dennie's editorship is known, however, and readers interested in particular identifications may consult Ellis, Queenan ("Appendix: Identification of Contributors"), Randall ("Authors of the *Port Folio* Revealed by the Hall Files"), and Kerber and Morris ("Politics and Literature: The Adams Family and *The Port Folio*").

For the study of literary Federalism as such, Lewis P. Simpson's "Federalism and the Crisis of Literary Order" (1960) remains seminal: "republic of letters" as it is employed in my discussion assumes Simpson's treatment of the idea of the *res publica literarum*. By the same token, Simpson's anthology *The Federalist Literary Mind* remains extremely valuable, suggesting the degree to which literary Federalism may to be seen as a single cultural outlook or system of values expressed in virtually identical terms in such separate publications as Dennie's *Port Folio* in Philadelphia and the *Monthly Anthology* in Boston. Taken together, Simpson's writings on Federalism still stand as a lonely beacon in our understanding of American literature in the early republic. Another ground-breaking work of older scholarship, the chapter on Washington Irving in Henry Seidel Canby's *Classic Americans* (1931), remains invaluable for under-standing the relationship between Dennie's literary Federalism and that of Irving and the *Salmagundi* group in New York.

The historical scholarship on Federalist politics in the Jeffersonian period is vast and, taken on its own terms, splendidly informative. Unfortunately, as a student of Dennie and the literary opposition to Jefferson soon learns, its terms do not often lead in any direct sense to an understanding of literary Federalism. So it is, for instance, that such otherwise exemplary studies as David Hackett Fischer's *The Revolution of American Conservatism* (1965) and James Banner's *To the Hartford Convention* (1970), or more specialized works such as George C. Rogers's fine biography of William Loughton Smith of Charleston (1962) and Forrest McDonald's *Alexander Hamilton* (1979), very often seem to a modern reader of *The Port Folio* only distantly and intermittently related to the world in which Dennie and his contributors thought and wrote. (Gerald Stourzh's *Alexander Hamilton* and the *Idea of Republican Government* [1970] is a partial exception, largely because it permits one to see how the "classical re-publican Hamilton" of *The Port Folio* could appear as such to Dennie and his readers.) In the same way, such admirable recent works as Gordon Wood's *The Radicalism of the American Revolution* (1992) or Elkins and McKitrick's *The Age of Federalism* (1993), even while subsuming earlier scholarship in the interests of larger-scale synthesis, have for reasons having to do with their focus tended to ignore the existence of literary Federalism. In literary studies proper, recent significant work by such scholars as Larzar Ziff and Jay Fliegelman has re-mained outside the purview of my discussion for similar reasons. The great ex-ception is Robert A. Ferguson's *Law and Letters in American Culture* (1984). In my notes, I have been content merely to remark several points of convergence with or divergence from Ferguson's interpretations; for the rest, my own argu-ment simply assumes the conclusions of his magisterial study.

In the existing historiography, three works stand out as being indispensable to any attempt to reconstruct the lost world of literary Federalism. The first is an established classic: Henry Adams's *History of the United States of America dur-ing the Administrations of Jefferson and Madison* (1889–1891). Historians have al-ways understood the greatness of this work; its depth and originality are, perhaps, just beginning to be fully appreciated by those working on the litera-ture of the early American republic. To a student of literary Federalism, its ad-ditional value lies in the special insight granted to Adams by his being able to draw on the papers of his family when these were otherwise unavailable. The second work most consistently useful to anyone working on literary Federal-ism is Linda K. Kerber's *Federalists in Dissent* (1970); though my conclusions differ from hers on several crucial points—most notably, the meaning of the debate over classical education—my own discussion is everywhere indebted to

Kerber's courageous and sympathetic attempt to show how anything so un-likely as a principled opposition to Jeffersonian democracy could have existed in the early American republic. In addition, the note on sources included at the end of Kerber's study gives a valuable overview of historical writing on the Federalists up to 1970. A third work, James Roger Sharp's *American Politics in the Early Republic* (1993), provided the analysis of party politics in the 1790s—a misnomer, technically, since its main point is that the concept of "party" was not yet intelligible during this period— that permitted me eventually to un-derstand several crucial features of literary Federalism.

Along with Dennie's letters and the contemporary memoirs and biogra-phies listed in my bibliography, there are also three works that seem to me to possess particular value for an understanding of *The Port Folio* in the years of Dennie's editorship. The first, Samuel Miller's *Memoir of the Reverend Charles Nisbet* (1840), is today read mainly by specialists. It is an account of the Scots-born first president of Dickinson College in Pennsylvania—a clergyman con-sidered in his native Scotland to have been a radical due to his support of the colonists in the American Revolution—who becomes, through a first-hand ac-quaintance with American backwoods democracy, a convert to Federalist prin-ciples. As a personal friend of Dennie's and a contributor to *The Port Folio*, Nisbet also played an important role in the development of literary Federalism. Miller's *Memoir*, in its own way a minor classic of early American biography, is an especially poignant introduction to the Nisbet one meets in the pages of Dennie's magazine.

The second work, known to every serious student of the early republic but too seldom sympathetically studied, is the two-volume edition of Fisher Ames's works published by Seth Ames in 1854. The value of Ames's writings for a student of literary Federalism is that there may be abstracted from them, in something like systematic form, the ideological grammar governing the ut-terance of Dennie and the *Port Folio* writers during their period of active oppo-sition to Jeffersonian democracy; this is how I have used Ames's *Works* in the present study. Yet their value to students of early republican literature, I have come to believe—and I have tried to suggest this by allowing Ames to speak "for" Federalism at various crucial moments—lies in his greatness as a thinker and writer. It has become customary to refer to Ames as "the American Burke." Yet despite one or two laudable recent attempts to understand him within the world of late classical republican values for which he was a last eloquent spokesman, we have yet fully to grasp, I think, the extent to which Ames really does stand in relation to early republican thought and writing as the Burke of *Reflections on the Revolution in France* or *Letter to a Noble Lord* does in relation to that of late-eighteenth-century England.

The third work most consistently useful to an attempt to make sense of lit-erary Federalism in its own terms is, I have found, Charles Downer Hazen's *Contemporary American Opinion of the French Revolution* (1897). The value of Hazen's work lies less in its ample use of primary sources—this has been duplicated or superseded in more recent specialized studies—than in its unwavering sense of how the French Revolution looked to those who had not yet learned to conceive of the world within the categories of Jeffersonian democratic ideology. This is the viewpoint most frequently and glaringly absent, it seems to me, not only from discussions of Dennie and *The Port Folio*, or even from wider discussions of Federalist politics, but from discussion of the early American republic generally.

My own argument concerning *The Port Folio* and literary Federalism runs athwart a much-controverted issue in the recent historiography of the early republic—namely, the question of whether Jefferson or his Federalist opponents have the more legitimate claim to represent the tradition of classical republican thought so splendidly recovered by J. G. A. Pocock in *The Machiavellian Moment* and related writings. As is well known, Jefferson's claims as a classical republican thinker have been developed by a particularly able group of historians. No matter where one stands in the controversy, it seems to me impossible to come away uninstructed from such a work as McCoy's *The Elusive Republic* (1980). As is also well known, the claims of such historians as McCoy and Banning have been brilliantly contested in a series of books and articles by Joyce Appleby. Though I have used all her works with intellectual profit, I have taken *Capitalism and a New Social Order* (1983), where Appleby seems to me to make most cogently the case for Federalists as the true classical republicans of the early American republic, as my most frequent point of reference in the foregoing pages.

My own position in the controversy will be evident to any reader of those pages. In brief, I think that the Jefferson one encounters in Banning's *The Jeffersonian Persuasion* (1978) or McCoy's *The Elusive Republic* does, if one takes the rhetoric of Jeffersonian democracy at face value, really exist; indeed, a reader of Dumas Malone's magisterial *Jefferson and His Time* (1948–1974) can scarcely doubt that this is the way Jefferson imagined himself. But the crucial fact is that the literary Federalists did not take such rhetoric at face value: to Dennie or Fisher Ames, Jefferson's "monstrous affectation of pure republicanism," as we have heard Ames call it, was very obviously mystification, an attempt to wrap the classical republican cloak of "primitive simplicity" (as Ames also says) around an ideology of unrestrained economic individualism. To a student of *The Port Folio*, the great value of Appleby's analysis is that it so penetratingly shows—even while she herself is drawing quite different conclusions about the moral and social implications of Jeffersonian ideology—how the Jefferson perceived by the literary Federalists could exist, how the apostle of primitive simplicity could be, wittingly or no, the first great ideologue of an emergent money or market society, and how it is possible responsibly to conclude that, as Gordon Wood has recently remarked, "for good or ill, American capitalism was created by American democracy" ("Enemy" 307). For all its brevity and the necessary rapidity of its analysis—the book consists of lectures originally given at New York University—*Capitalism and a New Social Order* seems to me the one genuinely indispensable work for an understanding of early republican literature and thought.

To the literary Federalists, as I have tried to show in chapter 1, the demystified truth of Jeffersonian ideology was land speculation—for them, the economic area where Jefferson's pretensions to agrarian simplicity most obviously intersected with the reality of America as a society wholly ruled by an ethic of what C. B. Macpherson famously called possessive individualism. Here again the historical literature is vast and complicated. The single best guide I have found to the Jeffersonian period viewed from this angle is Jacob E. Cooke's *Tenche Coxe and the Early Republic* (1978); the detailed bibliographical essay appended to Cooke's study is, in addition, an invaluable general guide to the historiography of Jeffersonian America. (For students of Dennie and *The Port Folio*, a special virtue is the detailed review of work on Jeffersonian party politics in Pennsylvania and New York.) Though written for a general rather than a scholarly audience, Daniel M. Friedenberg's *Life, Liberty, and the Pursuit of Land* (1993) in some ways operates as a valuable supplement to the more specialized studies of land speculation listed in Cooke's bibliography.

Finally, I should like to say something about why literary Federalism, if it really does constitute the crucial episode in American thought and writing claimed by my argument, should have remained so relatively invisible in American literary and intellectual history. The most obvious answer, that the triumph of Jeffersonian ideology was by the age of Andrew Jackson so complete as to have erased Federalism from the national memory, is a possibility already glimpsed in *The Port Folio* as early as 1804. There, one "Rusticus," having withdrawn to his private estate in an endeavor to escape the reality of Jeffersonian America, is disagreeing with a friend who has urged him to return to political combat. The friend's argument is a familiar one: though Federalism may have lost the temporary struggle, posterity will understand the legitimacy and urgency of its vision of America. But Rusticus foresees another possibility, which is that Jeffersonian ideology may triumph so completely that it will no longer be perceived as ideological—that is, for Americans, it may come simply to seem the truth about America. Whenever this has happened in previous epochs, observes Rusticus, the fate of the opposition has been simply to vanish from collective memory:

> You will urge me, to extend my views to distant ages . . . and to make 'the times to come my own.' But are you sure that even posthumous fame is always just? The opinion of posterity, may be less warped by prejudice, but it must necessarily be founded on testimony, and often on the testimony of interested witnesses. Have we not great reason to believe that the Carthaginian Heroes, have been cruelly misrepresented by the Roman Historians, and do we not know of many similar instances, in more modern times? When violent factions long prevail, errors, and prejudices, and falsehoods are likewise of long duration; they outlive the means of detection; their stains penetrate and discolour every page of History, and become at length indelible. (4:305)

Very recently, in light of certain revisionary energies that have for virtually the first time in two hundred years brought Jefferson back under genuinely critical scrutiny, we have begun to see how total has been the hegemony of Jeffersonian ideology in American civic life. Thus Gordon Wood, reviewing in the *New York Review of Books* a collected volume of papers from a recent conference: "More than any other of our so-called 'founding fathers' Jefferson has become a symbol, a touchstone, a measure of what we Americans are or where we are going. 'Jeffersonian' is a word of general appeal. We are continually asking ourselves whether Jefferson still survives, or what is still living in the thought of Jefferson; and we quote him on every side of every major issue in our history. No figure in our history has embodied so many of our hopes. Most Americans think of Jefferson much as our first professional biographer James Parton did. 'If Jefferson was wrong,' wrote Parton in 1874, 'America is wrong. If America is right, Jefferson was right.'" "If anything," adds Wood, "during these turbulent times the identification of Jefferson with America has become even greater (6)."

Recently, there have appeared two works that have challenged in crucial ways the entire received body of opinion about Jefferson: Joseph Ellis's *American Sphinx* (1997) and Conor Cruise O'Brien's *The Long Affair: Thomas Jefferson and the French Revolution* (1996). Readers of the two works will readily enough see the ways in which they converge with what Dennie and the *Port Folio* writers were so urgently trying to tell thoughtful Americans about Jeffersonian democracy in the early years of the nineteenth century. I will merely note in passing that Ellis's study, whatever historians ultimately decide about its merits as an appraisal of Jefferson, seems to me permanently valuable as a study specifically of what Ellis calls the capacity of Jeffersonian thought "to levitate out of its historical context" (298) so as to become the basis of a disembodied "American ideology." O'Brien's argument has been read by American scholars as too passionate and tendentious to be taken *sine grano salis*, especially as it insists on what one reviewer of the book calls the Stalinist streak in Jefferson's thought and temperament. My suspicion is that this is so entirely because O'Brien has come to Jefferson from a "European" perspective, and in particular from a long and deep study of the French Revolution and its subsequent influence on European thought. As someone who also came to the study of eighteenth-century American literature and thought from the European side, I can only say that O'Brien's estimate of Jefferson's relation to French radical thought seems to me highly persuasive and that I believe there will come a time when it is regarded as uncontroversial, even "standard," among those who study the early American republic.

By and large, however, I have tried in the present study to steer altogether clear of the "Jefferson controversy" among historians. The one partial exception concerns earlier writing on the period from the election of 1800 to Jackson's second term. No serious study of literary Federalism can get very far without becoming acutely aware of the degree to which a great deal of American historiography has been little more than an elaboration of Jeffersonian or Jacksonian ideology. Thus, for instance, the heroic frontiersman portrayed by Frederick Jackson Turner as the renewable source of American values is immediately recognizable to any reader of *The Port Folio* as the ragged backwoodsman already being proclaimed an avatar of the common man by

Jeffersonian democrats in Dennie's time. In the same way, a modern work such as Beard's *Economic Interpretation of the Constitution* would have been recognizable to the *Port Folio* writers as simply a late repetition of those attacks on an "aristocratical party" so tirelessly launched in their own time by Duane's *Aurora*. To the extent that I have drawn on the existing historiography in my own argument, therefore—and that has been, unavoidably, a very large extent—I have tried to correct in the interests of impartiality by treating the major works between Beard's *Economic Origins of Jeffersonian Democracy* and Schlesinger's *The Age of Jackson* less as history than as ideological self-celebration within the democratic republican tradition.

Selected Bibliography

Adams, Henry. *The History of the United States during the Administrations of Jefferson and Madison.* Ed. Earl N. Harbert. 2 vols. New York: Literary Classics of the United States, 1986.

Adams, J. Q. *American Principles: A Review of the Works of Fisher Ames.* Boston: Everett and Monroe, 1809.

———. *Lectures on Rhetoric and Oratory, Delivered to the Classes of Senior and Junior Sophisters in Harvard University.* Cambridge: Hilliard and Metcalf, 1810.

———. *Memoirs.* Philadelphia: J. B. Lippincott, 1876.

Adams, James Truslow. *New England in the Republic, 1776–1850.* Boston: Little, Brown, 1926.

Ames, Fisher. *Works.* Ed. Seth Ames, rev. W. B. Allen. 2 vols. Indianapolis: Liberty Classics, 1983.

Anderson, Benedict. *Imagined Communities: Reflections on the Origin and Spread of Nationalism.* London: Verso, 1991.

Anderson, Quentin. "Henry James's Cultural Office." In *Prospects: The Annual of American Cultural Studies.* Ed. Jack Salzman. Cambridge, England: Cambridge University Press, 1983.

———. *The Imperial Self.* New York: Knopf, 1971.

———. *Making Americans: An Essay on Individualism and Money.* New York: Harcourt, Brace, 1992.

Andrews, Charles M. *The Colonial Background of the American Revolution.* New Haven: Yale University Press, 1958.

Appleby, Joyce. "America as a Model for the Radical French Reformers of 1789." *William and Mary Quarterly* 28 (1971): 267–86.

———. *Capitalism and a New Social Order.* New York: New York University Press, 1983.

Selected Bibliography

———. "Commercial Farming and the 'Agrarian Myth' in the Early Republic." *Journal of American History* 68 (1982): 833–49.

———. *Economic Thought and Ideology in Seventeenth-Century England.* Princeton: Princeton University Press, 1978.

———. "What Is Still American in the Political Philosophy of Thomas Jefferson?" *William and Mary Quarterly* 39 (1982): 267–86.

Bailyn, Bernard. *The Ideological Origins of the American Revolution.* Cambridge: Harvard University Press, 1967.

Bailyn, ed. *The Great Republic.* Boston: Little, Brown, 1977.

Bailyn, ed. *Pamphlets of the American Revolution: 1750–1776.* Cambridge: Harvard University Press, 1965.

Banner, James M. *To the Hartford Convention: The Federalists and the Origins of Party Politics in Massachusetts, 1789–1815.* New York: Knopf, 1970.

Banning, Lance. *The Jeffersonian Persuasion.* Ithaca, N.Y.: Cornell University Press, 1978.

Beard, Charles. *Economic Origins of Jeffersonian Democracy.* New York: Macmillan, 1927.

Becker, Robert A. *Revolution, Reform and the Politics of American Taxation, 1763–1783.* Baton Rouge: Louisiana State University Press, 1980.

Beeman, Richard R. "The New Social History and the Search for 'Community' in Colonial America." *American Quarterly* 29 (1977): 422–43.

Beer, Samuel H. *To Make a Nation: the Rediscovery of American Federalism.* Cambridge: Harvard University Press, 1993.

Bernhard, Winfred E. A. *Fisher Ames: Federalist and Statesman, 1758–1808.* Chapel Hill: University of North Carolina Press, 1965.

Berthoff, Rowland. "Independence and Attachment, Virtue and Interest: From Republican Citizen to Free Enterpriser, 1787–1837." In *Uprooted Americans: Essays to Honor Oscar Handlin,* ed. Richard L. Bushman. Boston: Little, Brown, 1979.

Beveridge, A. J. *The Life of John Marshall.* Boston and New York: Houghton Mifflin, 1919.

Binney, Charles C. *The Life of Horace Binney.* Philadelphia: Lippincott and Company, 1903.

Blau, Joseph L. *American Philosophical Address, 1700–1900.* New York: Columbia University Press, 1946.

Boorstin, Daniel. *The Americans: The Colonial Experience.* New York: Random House, 1959.

Borden, Morton. *The Federalism of James A. Bayard.* New York: Columbia University Press, 1955.

———. *Parties and Politics in the Early Republic, 1789–1815.* New York: Crowell, 1967.

Breen, T. H. *Puritans and Adventurers: Change and Persistence in Early America.* New York: Oxford University Press, 1980.

Breisach, Ernst A. *American Progressive History.* Chicago: University of Chicago Press, 1993.

Brown, Chandos M. *Benjamin Silliman: A Life in the Young Republic*. Princeton: Princeton University Press, 1989.

Brown, David Paul. *The Forum, or Forty Years Field Practice at the Philadelphia Bar*. Philadelphia: R. H. Small, 1856.

Brown, Richard D. *The Strength of a People: The Idea of an Informed Citizenry in America, 1650–1870*. Chapel Hill: University of North Carolina Press, 1996.

Brown, Robert E. *Middle Class Democracy in Massachusetts and the Revolution*. Ithaca, N.Y.: Cornell University Press, 1955.

Buell, Lawrence. *New England Literary Culture*. New York: Cambridge University Press, 1986.

Burke, Edmund. *Reflections on the Revolution in France*. Ed. J. G. A. Pocock. Indianapolis: Hackett, 1987.

Bushman, Richard. *From Puritan to Yankee: Character and the Social Order in Connecticut, 1690–1765*. Cambridge: Harvard University Press, 1967.

Butterfield, Lyman, ed. *The Diary and Autobiography of John Adams*. 6 vols. Cambridge: Harvard University Press, 1961.

Cairns, William B. *British Criticisms of American Writings, 1783–1815*. University of Wisconsin Studies in Language and Literature, no. 1. Madison: University of Wisconsin Press, 1918.

Caldwell, Charles. *Autobiography*. Ed. Harriot W. Warner. Philadelphia: Lippincott, Grambo and Company, 1855.

Canby, Henry Seidel. *Classic Americans: A Study of Eminent American Writers from Irving to Whitman*. New York: Harcourt, Brace, 1931.

Cappon, Lester J., ed. *The Adams-Jefferson Letters*. 2 vols. Chapel Hill: University of North Carolina Press, 1959.

Cassell, Frank A. "The Structure of Baltimore's Politics in the Age of Jefferson, 1795–1812." In *Law, Society, and Politics in Early Maryland*, ed. Aubrey C. Land. Baltimore: Johns Hopkins University Press, 1977.

Charvat, William. *The Origins of American Critical Thought*. Philadelphia: University of Pennsylvania Press, 1936.

Cheetham, James. *A Dissertation Concerning Political Equality*. New York, 1800.

Childs, Frances Sergeant. *French Refugee Life in the United States, 1790–1800: An American Chapter of the French Revolution*. Baltimore: Johns Hopkins University Press, 1940.

Clark, Christopher. *The Roots of Rural Capitalism: Western Massachusetts, 1780–1860*. Ithaca, N.Y.: Cornell University Press, 1993.

Clark, David Lee. *Charles Brockden Brown*. Durham, N.C.: Duke University Press, 1952.

Cobbet, William. "Peter Porcupine." [see Wilson, David N.]

———. *A Year's Residence in the United States of America*. London: Sherwood, Neely, and Jones, 1818.

Cohen, William. "Thomas Jefferson and the Problem of Slavery." *Journal of American History* 56 (1969): 503–26.

Selected Bibliography

Cooke, Jacob E. "The Federalist Age: a Reappraisal." In George Athan Billias and Gerald N. Grob, eds., *American History: Retrospect and Prospect*. New York: Free Press, 1971.

———. *Tench Coxe and the Early Republic*. Chapel Hill: University of North Carolina Press, 1978.

Corner, George W., ed. *The Autobiography of Benjamin Rush*. Princeton: Princeton University Press, 1948.

Countryman, Edward. *A People in Revolution*. Baltimore: Johns Hopkins University Press, 1981.

Crosskey, W. W. *Politics and the Constitution*. 2 vols. Chicago: University of Chicago Press, 1953.

Cunningham, Noble. *The Process of Government under Jefferson*. Princeton: Princeton University Press, 1978.

Curti, Merle. *The Social Ideas of American Educators*. Chicago: Charles Scribner's Sons, 1935.

Dauer, Manning. *The Adams Federalists*. Baltimore: Johns Hopkins University Press, 1953.

Davidson, Cathy N. *Revolution and the Word: The Rise of the Novel in America*. New York: Oxford University Press, 1986.

Davis, John. *The Philadelphia Pursuits of Literature*. Philadelphia, 1805.

Davis, Richard Beale. *Intellectual Life in Jefferson's Virginia*. Chapel Hill: University of North Carolina Press, 1964.

DeConde, Alexander. *The Quasi-War: The Politics and Diplomacy of the Undeclared War with France: 1797–1801*. New York: Scribners, 1966.

Degler, Carl N. *Out of Our Past: The Forces that Shaped Modern America*. New York: Harper and Row, 1970.

Dennie, Joseph. *The Lay Preacher*. Ed. John E. Hall. Philadelphia: Harrison Hall, 1817.

———. *The Letters of Joseph Dennie*. Ed. Laura G. Pedder. *University of Maine Studies*, 2nd ser., 36. Orono, Maine, 1936.

Destler, C. M. *Joshua Coit, American Federalist, 1758–1798*. Middletown, Conn.: Wesleyan University Press, 1962.

Dowling, Linda. *Hellenism and Homosexuality in Victorian Oxford*. Ithaca, N.Y.: Cornell University Press, 1994.

Dowling, William C. *The Boswellian Hero*. Athens: University of Georgia Press, 1979.

———. *The Epistolary Moment: The Poetics of the Eighteenth-Century Verse Epistle*. Princeton: Princeton University Press, 1991.

———. *Poetry and Ideology in Revolutionary Connecticut*. Athens: University of Georgia Press, 1990.

Duane, William. "Letters of William Duane." *Proceedings of the Massachusetts Historical Society* 40 (1906–7): 257–394.

Dunn, John. "The Politics of Locke in England and America in the Eighteenth Century." In John W. Yolton, ed., *John Locke: Problems and Perspectives*. Cambridge: Cambridge University Press, 1969.

Dwight, Timothy. *Sermons*. 2 vols. New Haven, 1828.

———. *The True Means of Establishing Public Happiness*. New Haven, 1795.

East, Robert A. *John Quincy Adams: The Critical Years*. New York: Bookman Associates, 1962.

Elkins, Stanley, and McKitrick, Eric. *The Age of Federalism*. New York: Oxford University Press, 1993.

Ellis, Harold Milton. *Joseph Dennie and His Circle: A Study in American Literature from 1792 to 1812*. Austin: University of Texas Press, 1915.

Ellis, Joseph J. American *Sphinx: The Character of Thomas Jefferson*. New York: Knopf, 1997.

———. *Passionate Sage: The Character and Legacy of John Adams*. New York: Norton, 1993.

Ernst, Robert. *Rufus King: American Federalist*. Chapel Hill: University of North Carolina Press, 1968.

Ewing, Lucy E. Lee. *Doctor John Ewing and Some of His Noted Connections*. Philadelphia: John C. Winston, 1930.

Farrington, Benjamin. *The Faith of Epicurus*. New York: Basic Books, 1967.

Felt, Joseph B. *Memorials of William Smith Shaw*. Boston: S. K. Whipple and Company, 1852.

Ferguson, Robert A. *Law and Letters in American Culture*. Cambridge: Harvard University Press, 1984.

Fessenden, Thomas Green. *Democracy Unveiled, or Tyranny Stripped of the Garb of Patriotism* [by Christopher Caustic, L.L.D.]. 3d ed. New York, 1806.

Findley, William. *History of the Insurrection in the Four Western Counties of Pennsylvania*. Philadelphia, 1796.

Fischer, David Hackett. *The Revolution of American Conservatism: The Federalist Party in the Era of Jeffersonian Democracy*. New York: Harper and Row, 1965.

Flanagan, John T. *James Hall*. Minneapolis: University of Minnesota Press, 1941.

Flaumenhaft, Harvey. *The Effective Republic: Administration and Constitution in the Thought of Alexander Hamilton*. Durham: Duke University Press, 1992.

Foner, Philip S. *The Democratic-Republican Societies, 1790–1800*. Westport, Conn.: Greenwood Press, 1977.

Fox-Genovese, Elizabeth. *The Origins of Physiocracy*. Ithaca, N.Y.: Cornell University Press, 1976.

Freehling, William W. *The Road to Disunion*. New York: Oxford University Press, 1990.

Friedenberg, Daniel M. *Life, Liberty, and the Pursuit of Land: The Plunder of Early America*. Buffalo, N.Y.: Prometheus, 1993.

Friedrich, Carl J. *Nomos IV: Liberty: Yearbook of the American Society for Political and Legal Philosophy*. New York: Atherton Press, 1962.

Fussell, Paul. *The Rhetorical World of Augustan Humanism*. Oxford: Clarendon Press, 1965.

Gibbs, George. *Memoirs of the Administrations of Washington and John Adams, Edited from the Papers of Oliver Wolcott*. New York: W. Van Norden, 1846.

Goodfellow, Donald Munro. *The Literary Life of John Quincy Adams.* Ph.D. dissertation. Harvard University, 1944.

Goodnight, Scott Holland. *German Literature in American Magazines Prior to 1846. Bulletin of the University of Wisconsin* 188. Madison: University of Wisconsin Press, 1907.

Govan, Thomas R. "The Death of Joseph Dennie: A Memoir by Nicholas Biddle." *Pennsylvania Magazine of History and Biography* 75 (1951): 36–46.

Graydon, Alexander. *Memoirs of a Life Chiefly Passed in Pennsylvania within the Last Sixty Years.* Harrisburg: Printed by John Wyeth, 1811.

Greene, Jack P. *Pursuits of Happiness: The Social Development of Early Modern British Colonies and the Formation of American Culture.* Chapel Hill: University of North Carolina Press, 1988.

———. "The Social Origins of the American Revolution: An Evaluation and an Interpretation." *Political Science Quarterly* 88 (1973): 1–24.

Habermas, Jurgen. *The Structural Transformation of the Public Sphere.* Trans. Thomas Burger. Cambridge: MIT Press, 1989.

Hall, James. "Memoir of Mrs. Sarah Hall." In *Selections from the Writings of Mrs. Sarah Hall.* Ed. John Hall. Philadelphia: Harrison Hall, 1833.

Hall, John E. *The Philadelphia Souvenir.* Philadelphia: Harrison Hall, 1827.

Hall, Sarah. *Selections from the Writings of Mrs. Sarah Hall.* Ed. John Hall. Philadelphia: Harrison Hall, 1833.

Hall, Van Beck. *Politics without Parties: Masschusetts, 1780–1791.* Pittsburgh: University of Pittsburgh Press, 1972.

Hamilton, Alexander. [see Syrett, Harold]

Hansen, Allen Oscar. *Liberalism and American Education in the Eighteenth Century.* New York: Macmillan, 1926.

Hartz, Louis. *The Liberal Tradition in American History.* New York: Harcourt Brace, 1955.

Hatch, Nathan O. *The Sacred Cause of Liberty: Republican Thought and the Millennium in Revolutionary New England.* New Haven: Yale University Press, 1977.

Hayek, F. A., ed. *Capitalism and the Historians.* Chicago: University of Chicago Press, 1954.

Hazen, Charles Downer. *Contemporary American Opinion of the French Revolution.* Baltimore: Johns Hopkins University Press, 1897.

Hedges, William L. *Washington Irving: An American Study—1802–1832.* Baltimore: Johns Hopkins University Press, 1965.

Heimert, Alan. *Religion and the American Mind.* Cambridge: Harvard University Press, 1966.

Henretta, James A. *The Evolution of American Society, 1700–1815.* Lexington, Mass.: Heath, 1973.

———. *The Origins of American Capitalism.* Boston: Northeastern University Press, 1993.

Hoffer, Peter C. "The Constitutional Crisis and the Rise of a Nationalistic View of History in America, 1786–1788." *New York History* 52 (1971): 311–17.

Hofstader, Richard. *The Age of Reform.* New York: Knopf, 1955.

———. *The Idea of a Party System: The Rise of Legitimate Opposition in the United States, 1780–1840.* Berkeley: University of California Press, 1969.

Howard, Leon. *The Connecticut Wits.* Chicago: University of Chicago Press, 1943.

———. "Wordsworth in America." *Modern Language Notes* 48 (1933): 359–65.

Howe, M. A. DeWolfe, ed. "Journal of Josiah Quincy, Jr., 1773." *Proceedings of the Massachusetts Historical Society* 49 (1916): 425–81.

Ingersoll, Charles Jared. *Inchiquin, The Jesuit's Letters.* New York: I. Riley, 1810.

———. *A View of the Rights and Wrongs, Power and Policy, of the United States of America.* Philadelphia: O. and A. Conrad and Company, 1808.

Isaac, Rhys. *The Transformation of Virginia, 1740–1790.* Chapel Hill: University of North Carolina Press, 1982.

Jackson, Joseph. *Literary Landmarks of Philadelphia.* Philadelphia: David McKay, 1939.

Jehlen, Myra. *American Incarnation: The Individual, the Nation, and the Continent.* Cambridge: Harvard University Press, 1986.

Johnson, James William. "The Meaning of 'Augustan.'" *Journal of the History of Ideas* 19 (1958): 507–22.

Jones, Howard M. *American and French Culture, 1750–1848.* Chapel Hill: University of North Carolina Press, 1927.

Jordan, Winthrop D. *White over Black: American Attitudes toward the Negro, 1550–1812.* Chapel Hill: University of North Carolina Press, 1968.

Josephson, Matthew. *Portrait of the Artist as American.* New York: Farrar, Straus, and Giroux, 1979 [1930].

Keller, Charles Roy. *The Second Great Awakening in Connecticut.* New Haven: Yale University Press, 1942.

Kelley, Robert. "Ideology and Political Culture from Jefferson to Nixon." *American Historical Review* 82 (June 1977): 531–62.

Kellogg, Thelma Louise. *The Life and Works of John Davis, 1774–1853. University of Maine Studies,* 2d ser., 1. Orono, Maine, 1924.

Kenyon, Cecelia. "Alexander Hamilton: Rousseau of the Right." *Political Science Quarterly* 73 (1958): 161–78.

Kerber, Linda K. *Federalists in Dissent: Imagery and Ideology in Jeffersonian America.* Ithaca, N.Y.: Cornell University Press, 1970.

Kerber and Morris, Walter John. "Politics and Literature: The Adams Family and the Port Folio." *William and Mary Quarterly* 23 (1966): 450–78.

King, Charles R., ed. *The Life and Correspondence of Rufus King.* 6 vols. New York: G. P. Putnam's Sons, 1895.

Kinloch, Francis. *Letters from Geneva and France.* Boston, 1819.

Koch, Gustav Adolf. *Republican Religion: The American Revolution and the Cult of Reason*. New York: Henry Holt and Company, 1933.

Korngold, Ralph. *Citizen Toussaint*. London: Gollancz, 1945.

Kramnick, Isaac. "Republican Revisionism Revisited." *American Historical Review* 87 (1982): 629–64.

———. *Republicanism and Bourgeois Radicalism in Late Eighteenth-Century England and America*. Ithaca, N.Y.: Cornell University Press, 1990.

Kulikoff, Allan. *The Agrarian Origins of American Capitalism*. Charlottesville: University Press of Virginia, 1993.

Kurtz, Stephen G. *The Presidency of John Adams: The Collapse of Federalism*. Philadelphia: University of Pennsylvania Press, 1957.

Leary, Lewis. "John Blair Linn, 1777–1805." *William and Mary Quarterly* 9 (1947): 148–76.

———. "Joseph Dennie on Benjamin Franklin." *Pennsylvania Magazine of History and Biography* 72 (1948): 240–46.

———. "Leigh Hunt in Philadelphia." *Pennsylvania Magazine of History and Biography* 70 (1946): 270–80.

Lee, Robert Edson. "Timothy Dwight and the Boston *Palladium*." *New England Quarterly* 35 (1962): 229–39.

Lerner, Ralph. *Revolutions Revisited: Two Faces of the Politics of Enlightenment*. Chapel Hill: University of North Carolina Press, 1994.

Lippincott, Horace Mather. *Early Philadelphia: Its People, Life and Progress*. Philadelphia: J. B. Lippincott Company, 1917.

Litto, Fredric M. "Addison's *Cato* in the Colonies." *William and Mary Quarterly* 23 (1966): 431–49.

Lizanich, Christine M. "'The March of this Government': Joel Barlow's Unwritten History of the United States." *William and Mary Quarterly* 33 (1976): 318–23.

Lochemes, Sister Mary Frederick. *Robert Walsh, His Story*. Washington, D.C.: Catholic University of America Press, 1941.

Logan, George. *An Address on the Natural and Social Order*. Philadelphia: Benjamin Franklin Bache, 1798.

Luxon, Niel Norval. *Niles' Weekly Register*. Baton Rouge: Louisiana State University Press, 1947.

Mack, Maynard. *The Garden and the City: Retirement and Politics in the Later Poetry of Pope*. Toronto: University of Toronto Press, 1969.

Magrath, C. Peter. *Yazoo: Law and Politics in the New Republic*. Providence, R.I.: Brown University Press, 1966.

Maier, Pauline. "Popular Uprisings and Civil Authority in Eighteenth-Century America." *William and Mary Quarterly* 27 (1970): 3–35.

Main, Jackson Turner. *Political Parties before the Constitution*. Chapel Hill: University of North Carolina Press, 1973.

———. *The Social Structure of Revolutionary America*. Princeton: Princeton University Press, 1965.

Malone, Dumas. *Jefferson and His Time*. 5 vols. Boston: Little, Brown, 1948–1974.

——. *The Public Life of Thomas Cooper, 1783–1839*. New Haven: Yale University Press, 1925.

Malsberger, John W. "The Political Thought of Fisher Ames." *Journal of the Early Republic* 2 (1982): 1–20.

Matthiessen, F. O. *Theodore Dreiser*. New York: William Sloan, 1951.

Mayo, Thomas Franklin. *Epicurus in England*. Ph.D. diss., Columbia University, 1993.

McColley, Robert. *Slavery and Jeffersonian Virginia*. Urbana: University of Illinois Press, 1964.

McCoy, Drew R. *The Elusive Republic*. Chapel Hill: University of North Carolina Press, 1980.

McDonald, Forrest. *Alexander Hamilton: A Biography*. New York: Norton, 1979.

McInerney, Daniel J. *The Fortunate Heirs of Freedom: Abolition and Republican Thought*. Lincoln: University of Nebraska Press, 1994.

Meigs, William W. *The Life of Charles Jared Ingersoll*. Philadelphia: J. B. Lippincott, 1897.

Mesick, Jane Louise. *The English Traveller in America, 1785–1835*. New York: Columbia University Press, 1922.

Meyers, Marvin. *The Jacksonian Persuasion*. Palo Alto: Stanford University Press, 1957.

Miles, Gary B. *Virgil's Georgics*. Berkeley: University of California Press, 1980.

Miller, John C. *Alexander Hamilton: Portrait in Paradox*. New York: Harper, 1959.

Miller, Samuel. *Memoir of the Reverend Charles Nisbet, D. D.* New York, 1840.

Moore, Thomas. *Memoirs, Journal and Correspondence*. Ed. Lord John Russell. London: Longmans, 1856.

——. *Poetical Works*. 10 vols. New York: D. Appleton, 1853.

——. "Two Letters from Thomas Moore to Joseph Dennie." *Critic* (2 June 1888): 270.

Morgan, Edmund S. *Inventing the People: The Rise of Popular Sovereignty in England and America*. New York: Norton, 1988.

Morris, Richard B., ed. *Alexander Hamilton and the Founding of the Nation*. New York: Dial, 1957.

Mott, Frank Luther. *A History of American Magazines, 1741–1850*. New York: D. Appleton and Company, 1930.

Murrin, John M. "The Great Inversion, or Court versus Country: A Comparison of the Revolution Settlements in England (1688–1721) and America (1776–1816). In J. G. A. Pocock, ed., *Three British Revolutions: 1641, 1688, 1776*. Princeton: Princeton University Press, 1980.

——. "The Myths of Colonial Democracy and Royal Decline in Eighteenth-Century America." *Cithara* 5 (1965).

Nash, Gary B. "The American Clergy and the French Revolution." *William and Mary Quarterly* 22 (1965): 392–412.

———. "The Transformation of Urban Politics 1700–1765." *Journal of American History* 60 (1973): 605–32.

———. *The Urban Crucible*. Cambridge: Harvard University Press, 1979.

Neal, John. *Wandering Recollections of a Somewhat Busy Life*. Boston: Roberts Brothers, 1869.

Nelson, John R. "Alexander Hamilton and American Manufacturing: A Reexamination." *Journal of American History* 65 (1978–1979): 971–95.

Nettels, Curtis P. *The Emergence of a National Economy: 1775–1815*. New York: Holt, 1962.

Nuermberger, R. K. "Asbury Dickins." *North Carolina Historical Review* 24 (1947): 281–314.

Nye, Russel B. *The Cultural Life of the New Nation*. New York: Harper, 1960.

Oberholtzer, Ellis Paxson. *The Literary History of Philadelphia*. Philadelphia: G. W. Jacobs and Company, 1906.

———. *Philadelphia: A History of the City and Its People*. 4 vols. Philadelphia, n.d.

O'Brien, Conor Cruise. *The Long Affair: Thomas Jefferson and the French Revolution*. Chicago: University of Chicago Press, 1996.

Onuf, Peter S., ed. *Jeffersonian Legacies*. Charlottesville: University Press of Virginia, 1993.

Parrington, Vernon. *Main Currents of American Thought*. 3 vols. New York: Harcourt, Brace, 1927–1930.

Passmore, John. *The Perfectibility of Man*. London: Duckworth, 1970.

Paulding, James Kirke. *The United States and England*. New York: Van Winkle and Wiley, 1815.

Perrin, Porter Gale. *The Life and Works of Thomas Green Fessenden*. *University of Maine Studies*, 2d ser., 4. Orono, Maine, 1925.

Persons, Stow. "The Cyclical Theory of History in Eighteenth-Century America." *American Quarterly* 6 (1954): 147–63.

Peterson, Merrill D. *The Jeffersonian Image in the American Mind*. New York: Oxford University Press, 1960.

———. Review of volumes 18 and 19 of *The Papers of Thomas Jefferson*. *William and Mary Quarterly* 32 (1975):656–58.

———. *Thomas Jefferson and the New Nation*. New York: Oxford University Press, 1979.

Pocock, J. G. A. *The Machiavellian Moment*. Princeton: Princeton University Press, 1975.

Poirier, Richard. *A World Elsewhere: The Place of Style in American Literature*. Madison: University of Wisconsin Press, 1985.

Pole, J. R. *The Pursuit of Equality in American History*. Berkeley: University of California Press, 1978.

Powell, J. B. *Richard Rush: Republican Democrat, 1780–1859*. Philadelphia: University of Pennsylvania Press, 1948.

Prince, Carl E. "The Passing of the Aristocracy: Jefferson's Removal of the Federalists," 1801–1805." *Journal of American History* 67 (1970): 573–75.

Purcell, James B. *Literary Culture in North Carolina before 1820*. Ph.D. diss., Duke University, 1950.

Purcell, Richard J. *Connecticut in Transition, 1775–1818*. Middletown, Conn.: Wesleyan University Press, 1963.

Queenan, John T. "*The Port Folio*: A Study of the History and Significance of an Early American Magazine." Ph.D diss. University of Pennsylvania, 1954.

Quincy, Edmund. *The Life of Josiah Quincy*. Boston: Ticknor and Fields, 1867.

Quincy, Josiah. "Account of Journey of Josiah Quincy." *Proceedings of the Massachusetts Historical Society*, 2d ser., 4 (1888): 123–35.

Rahe, Paul A. *Republics Ancient and Modern: Classical Republicanism and the American Revolution*. Chapel Hill: University of North Carolina Press, 1992.

Randall, Randolph C. "Authors of the *Port Folio* Revealed by the Hall Files." *American Literature* 11 (1940): 379–416.

Richard, Carl J. *The Founders and the Classics: Greece, Rome, and the American Enlightenment*. Cambridge: Harvard University Press, 1994.

Risjord, Norman K. "The Virginia Federalists." *Journal of Southern History* 33 (1967): 486–517.

Robinson, Blackwell P. *William R. Davie*. Chapel Hill: University of North Carolina Press, 1957.

Robinson, William Alexander. "The Washington Benevolent Society in New England: A Phase of Politics during the War of 1812." *Proceedings of the Massachusetts Historical Society* 49 (1916): 274–86.

Rogers, George C. *Evolution of a Federalist: William Loughton Smith of Charleston (1758–1812)*. Columbia: University of South Carolina Press, 1962.

Rosenmeyer, Thomas. *The Green Cabinet*. Berkeley: University of California Press, 1969.

Rõstvig, Maren-Sofie. *The Happy Man: Studies in the Metamorphoses of a Classical Ideal*. 2 vols. Vol 1: 1600–1700. Oslo: Akademisk forlag, 1954. Vol. 2: 1700–1760. Oslo: Oslo University Press, 1958.

Rothenberg, Winifred Barr. *From Market-Places to a Market Economy: The Transformation of Rural Massachusetts, 1750–1850*. Chicago: University of Chicago Press, 1993.

Royster, Charles. *A Revolutionary People at War: The Continental Army and American Character, 1775–1783*. Chapel Hill: University of California Press, 1989.

Rubin-Dorsky, Jeffry. *Adrift in the Old World: The Psychological Pilgrimage of Washington Irving*. Chicago: University of Chicago Press, 1988.

Rush, Benjamin. [see Corner, G. W.]

Sansom, Joseph. *Travels from Paris through Switzerland and Italy, 1801–2*. London: R. Phillips, 1808.

Santayana, George. [See Wilson, Douglas L.]

Schlesinger, Arthur M., Jr. *The Age of Jackson*. Boston: Little, Brown, 1946.

Schwoerer, Lois G. *The Declaration of Rights, 1689*. Baltimore: Johns Hopkins University Press, 1982.

Scudder, Horace E. *Noah Webster*. Boston: Houghton Mifflin, 1899.

Sellers, Charles. *The Market Revolution: Jacksonian America, 1815–1846*. New York: Oxford University Press, 1991.

Sellers, M. N. S. *American Republicanism: Roman Ideology in the United States Constitution*. New York: New York University Press, 1994.

Seneca. *The Stoic Philosophy of Seneca*. Trans. Moses Hadas. New York: Norton, 1958.

Shalhope, Robert E. "Republicanism and Early American Historiography." *William and Mary Quarterly* 39 (1982): 334–56.

———. "Thomas Jefferson's Republicanism and Antebellum Southern Thought." *Journal of Southern History* 42 (1976): 529–56.

Sharp, James Roger. *American Politics in the Early Republic: The New Nation in Crisis*. New Haven: Yale University Press, 1993.

Shoemaker, Ervin C. *Noah Webster: Pioneer of Learning*. New York: Columbia University Press, 1936.

Shoemaker, Robert W. "'Democracy' and 'Republic' as Understood in Late Eighteenth-Century America." *American Speech* 41 (1966): 83–95.

Simpson, Lewis P. "Federalism and the Crisis of Literary Order," *American Literature* 32 (1960).

———. "A Literary Adventure of the Early Republic: The Anthology Society and the Monthly Anthology." *New England Quarterly* 27(1954): 168–90.

———. "The Symbolism of Literary Alienation in the Revolutionary Age." In *The Brazen Face of History: Studies in the Literary Consciousness in America*. Baton Rouge: Louisiana State University Press, 1980.

Simpson, ed. *The Federalist Literary Mind: Selections from the Monthly Anthology and Boston Review, 1803–1811*. Baton Rouge: Louisiana State University Press, 1962.

Sisson, Daniel. *The American Revolution of 1800*. New York: Knopf, 1974.

Smith, Edgar Fahs. *The Life of Robert Hare*. Philadelphia: J. B. Lippincott Company, 1917.

Smith, James Morton. *Freedom's Fetters*. Ithaca, N.Y.: Cornell University Press, 1956.

Smyth, Albert H. *The Philadelphia Magazines and Their Contributors, 1741–1850*. Philadelphia: Robert M. Lindsay, 1892.

Spencer, Benjamin T. *The Quest for Nationality: An American Literary Campaign*. Syracuse, N.Y.: Syracuse University Press, 1957.

Spiller, Robert E., ed. *The American Literary Revolution, 1783–1837*. New York: Anchor Books, 1967.

Stewart, Donald H. *The Opposition Press of the Federalist Period*. Albany: SUNY Press, 1969.

Stirk, S. D. "John Quincy Adams's Letters on Silesia." *New England Quarterly* 9 (1936): 485–99.

Stourzh, Gerald. *Alexander Hamilton and the Idea of Republican Government*. Palo Alto: Stanford University Press, 1970.

Surrency, Erwin C. "The Judiciary Act of 1801." *American Journal of Legal History* 2 (1958): 54–65.

Sydnor, Charles S. *Gentlemen Freeholders.* Chapel Hill: University of North Carolina Press, 1952.

Syrett, Harold, ed. *The Papers of Alexander Hamilton.* 26 vols. New York: Columbia University Press, 1974.

Tagg, James. *Benjamin Franklin Bache and the Philadelphia Aurora.* Philadelphia: University of Pennsylvania Press, 1991.

Tanselle, G. Thomas. *Royall Tyler.* Cambridge: Harvard University Press, 1967.

Tansill, Charles Callen. *The United States and Santo Domingo, 1798–1873.* Baltimore: Johns Hopkins University Press, 1938.

Tassin, Algernon. *The Magazine in America.* New York: Dodd, Mead, and Company, 1916.

Taylor, Charles. *Philosophical Arguments.* Cambridge: Harvard University Press, 1995.

Thoreau, Henry David. *Walden.* Boston: Houghton, Mifflin, 1906.

Thorp, Willard, ed. *The Lives of Eighteen from Princeton.* Princeton: Princeton University Press, 1946.

Tinkcom, Harry Martin. *The Republicans and Federalists in Pennsylvania, 1790–1801.* Harrisburg: Pennsylvania Historical Commission, 1950.

Tocqueville, Alexis de. *L'ancien regime et la Revolution.* Ed. J-P Mayer. Paris: Gallimard, 1967.

Tucker, George. *Essays on Various Subjects of Taste, Morals, and National Policy.* Georgetown, D.C.: J. Milligan, 1822.

Tupper, Frederick, and Brown, Helen Tyler, eds. *Grandmother Tyler's Book.* New York: G. P. Putnam's Sons, 1925.

Turner, Frederick Jackson. "Contributions of the West to American Democracy." *Atlantic Monthly* 91 (January 1903): 79–76.

Turner, Kathryn. "Federalist Policy and the Judiciary Act of 1801." *William and Mary Quarterly* 22 (1965): 3–32.

Twomey, Richard Jerome. "Jacobins and Jeffersonians: Anglo-American Radical Ideology, 1790–1810." In *The Origins of Anglo-American Radicalism,* ed. Margaret C. Jacob and James R. Jacob. London: Allen and Unwin, 1983.

Tyler, Mary Palmer. [see Tupper, Frederick, and Brown, Helen Tyler]

Upham, Charles W. *The Life of Timothy Pickering.* Boston: Little, Brown, 1873.

Ver Steeg, Clarence. *Robert Morris: Revolutionary Financier.* Philadelphia: University of Pennsylvania Press, 1954.

Waln, Robert. *The Hermit in America on a Visit to Philadelphia.* Philadelphia: M. Thomas, 1819.

———. *The Hermit in Philadelphia.* Philadelphia: M. Thomas, 1821.

———. *Sisyphi Opus.* Philadelphia: J. Maxwell and Moses Thomas, 1820.

Walsh, Robert. *An Appeal from the Judgments of Great Britain Respecting the United States of America.* Philadelphia: Mitchell, Ames and White, 1819.

———. *Didactics.* Philadelphia: Carey, Lea and Blanchard, 1836.

Walters, Kerry S. *Rational Infidels: The American Deists.* Durango, Colo.: Longwood Academic, 1992.

Warfel, Harry. *Charles Brockden Brown.* Gainesville: University of Florida Press, 1949.

———. *Noah Webster, Schoolmaster to America.* New York: Macmillan, 1936.

Warner, Michael. *The Letters of the Republic: Publication and the Public Sphere in Eighteenth-Century America.* Cambridge: Harvard University Press, 1990.

Washburn, Charles Greenfield, ed. "Letters of Thomas Boylston Adams to William Smith Shaw, 1799–1823." *Proceedings of the American Antiquarian Society.* New ser. 27 (1917): 83–176.

Watts, Steven. *The Republic Reborn: War and the Making of Liberal America, 1790–1820.* Baltimore: Johns Hopkins University Press, 1987.

Weimer, Albert B. *Reports of Cases Adjudged in the Supreme Court of Pennsylvania by the Honorable Jasper Yeates.* Philadelphia: T. J. Johnson and Company, 1890.

Welch, Richard E. *Theodore Sedgwick, Federalist: A Political Portrait.* Middletown, Conn.: Wesleyan University Press, 1965.

Welter, Rush. *Popular Education and Democratic Thought in America.* New York: Columbia University Press, 1962.

Wendell, Barrett. *A Literary History of America.* New York: Greenwood Press, 1968.

Wheeler, William O. *The Ogden Family in America.* Philadelphia: J. B. Lippincott Company, 1907.

White, Leonard D. *The Federalists: A Study in Administration History.* New York: Macmillan, 1948.

White, Morton. *The Philosophy of the American Revolution.* Oxford: Oxford University Press, 1978.

Wills, Garry. *Inventing America: Jefferson's Declaration of Independence.* New York: Doubleday, 1978.

Wilson, David A., ed. *Peter Porcupine in America: Pamphlets on Republicanism and Revolution by William Cobbett.* Ithaca, N.Y.: Cornell University Press, 1994.

Wilson, Douglas L., ed. *The Genteel Tradition: Nine Essays by George Santayana.* Cambridge: Harvard University Press, 1967.

Wood, Gordon. *The Creation of the American Republic.* Chapel Hill: University of North Carolina Press, 1969.

———. "The Enemy Is Us: Democratic Capitalism in the Early Republic." *Journal of the Early Republic* 16, no. 2 (Summer 1996): 293–308.

———. "A Note on Mobs in the American Revolution." *William and Mary Quarterly* 23 (1966): 635–42.

———. *The Radicalism of the American Revolution.* New York: Knopf, 1992.

———. Review of *Jeffersonian Legacies,* ed. Peter Onuf. *The New York Review of Books* 40, no. 9 (13 May 1993), 6–9.

Wood, James Playsted. *Magazines in the United States.* New York: Ronald Press, 1949.

Young, Alfred F. *The Democratic Republicans of New York: The Origins, 1763–1797*. Chapel Hill: University of North Carolina Press, 1967.

Ziff, Larzer. *Writing in the New Nation*. New Haven: Yale University Press, 1991.

Zuckerman, Michael. *Peaceable Kingdoms: New England Towns in the Eighteenth Century*. New York: Knopf, 1970.

Zvesper, John. *Political Philosophy and Rhetoric: A Study of the Origins of American Party Politics*. Cambridge: Harvard University Press, 1977.

Index

Index

Washington, George, 2, 8, 13, 22, 32–33, 41–42, 84; and classical republican *virtus*, 33–34; as Leonidas, 32

Whiskey Rebellion, 24

Wills, Garry, 9

Wilson, Alexander, 24–25

Windham, William, 43, 46–47

Wollstonecraft, Mary, 8

Wood, Gordon, 4, 39